FIGHTERS IN DEFENCE

MEMORIES OF THE GLASGOW SQUADRON

by

Hector MacLean

Copyright © C Hector MacLean 1999

'Battle of Britain' – 'Gauntlet' Copyright © Anthony Saunders.
Limited Edition Prints available from Cranston Fine Arts.
Tel: 01436 820269

First published in Great Britain in 1999
by Squadron Prints Ltd

MacLean, Hector
Fighters in Defence, memories of the Glasgow Squadron
1. Great Britain. Royal Air Force
1. Title
358.4'

ISBN 0 95126 561 X

Designed and produced by
Alan Carlaw, Squadron Prints Ltd
Giffnock, Glasgow G46 7LT, Scotland

Printed in Great Britain by
Elpeeko Ltd, Lincoln LN2 4JY

Charles Hector Maclean

For my son

Captain Marcus MacLean

CONTENTS

Air experience with "Hoddy"
MacLean in Wapiti I, Renfrew 1933
Painting by Dugald Cameron

FOREWORD

by

AIR VICE-MARSHAL A V R JOHNSTONE, CB DFC AE DL

Whatever Hector MacLean has to say, or has written about, is worth studying. After all he has a trained legal mind which, combined with boundless energy and an indomitable spirit, puts him in a class of his own. I should know, for Hector and I 'learned' our flying together in the mid-thirties and have remained good friends ever since.

Being a member of No. 602 Squadron, Auxiliary Air Force, since pre-war days was a privilege not given to many. Although regarded at the time by many Regular Units of the Royal Air Force as no more than playboys of the privileged, the Auxiliaries gave them a rude awakening in the early days of World War, when 602 Squadron and its sister Squadron from Edinburgh accounted for the first enemy aircraft shot down over British soil. From then on the Regulars were tumbling over themselves to join us in Scotland to find out what true thirties aerial fighting was all about! MacLean's recollections of those early days make fascinating reading and add lustre to an important period in the nation's history.

When the Battle of Britain was being fought, 602 Squadron was naturally in the thick of it. It was a sad day for me while in command of that famous unit when Hector's Spitfire stopped an explosive cannon shell from an Me 109 fighter escorting German bombers returning from a heavy raid on Portsmouth. He was left to fly back a badly damaged aeroplane without a rudder and with his right foot dangling in its shoe, hanging by the remains of his ankle. After landing at Tangmere with his wheels up MacLean was able to drag himself to safety from the cockpit on to the ground. I visited my erstwhile Flight Commander in hospital two days later by which time the leg had been amputated below the knee. I found him propped up by pillows already appreciating the attentions of the prettier nurses. As to the leg it had been a painful way of achieving the day off he hadn't had since we had got down there! Such is the calibre of the Author!

Unable to return to active flying duties for the time being, MacLean wasted no time being trained as a Fighter Controller on the ground, where his front-line experience in the air could be put to maximum effect. In this sphere, too, he was soon to make his mark and there are still many fighter pilots who owe the outcome of successful victories to the wise and imaginative guidance they received in the capable hands of Hector MacLean now, to his personal chagrin, forced to take charge of affairs from the fastness of a Fighter Operations Room.

The exploits of those privileged to fly Spitfires and Hurricanes during the Battle of Britain found themselves 'hitting the headlines' and being feted wherever they went. But, let us face it - they were only the fellows at the sharp end of the conflict whose sole job was to fire bullets at our unwelcome visitors from an opposing force. Someone had to load the bullets into the aircraft in the first place, whilst others had to produce them. Meanwhile the Nation had to be sustained. The vital roles played by the men of the Royal and Merchant Navies were every bit as important; as indeed was the fortitude of the hundreds of thousand civilians who carried on with their ground jobs in spite of being subjected to continual bombing day after day and night after night. Everyone had a special part to play in this, now historic, battle. Among the most important of these was the small band of well-trained officers, airmen and airwomen whose responsibility was to guide our fighter aircraft on to the incoming raiders, hopefully before they could start wrecking too much havoc on their intended targets. I often feel that not enough credit has been given to this most important part of our air defence system and it is refreshing to read of MacLean's personal experiences while serving in it. This book is a long overdue tribute; and who better to expound it than one who first distinguished himself as a combat pilot in the air and who, later, was able to apply that priceless experience to guide, from the ground, the 'derring-do' who were to follow him into the unknown. Some of his views may be unorthodox but they are none the worse for that!

INTRODUCTION

Although much of this work recalls my service with 602 City of Glasgow Squadron it is not intended as a Squadron history. Thanks to several published books written as a result of devoted research including those by Douglas MacRoberts and Professor Dugald Cameron, the history of 602 Squadron in the Second World War has been well documented. A personal account of the Squadron during the period in which I served could be of interest to my family, but is unlikely to add significantly to the principal facts already so faithfully recorded by those dedicated authors; but I do have the advantage of having lived through that exciting period of our lives and can, hopefully, bring to life and memory some of the characters about whom little has been written, and who played their part, not just in the air, but also on the ground.

Fortunately for posterity Sandy Johnstone, who served in the Squadron during my time and beyond, kept a diary recorded verbatim in his book "Spitfire into War" published in 1986. His account of the Squadron during the defensive phase of its operations, as the events took place, trumps most of what I can add nearly sixty years later; so would there be any point in publishing a story that had already been so well told? However Sandy himself had been, from the outset, a B Flight pilot, and so remained until 11th July 1940 when he took command of the Squadron. I could, therefore, fill in some of the gaps and a little more about the other half of the Squadron which consisted of A Flight in which I served from 17th November 1935 until 26th August 1940 when my contribution came to an abrupt end in St Richards Hospital, Chichester.

Having been present and personally involved during four years before the war and during the first year of the Squadron's operations, there are some remaining gaps which I can fill. A personal story seemed to me a readable way of recalling and explaining the events which took place during that period.

My original purpose was to recall early days in the Squadron before and during the first year of the war with some character sketches coupled with my own experiences in the air; also the men I encountered, and the events in which I took part. As the work progressed it dawned on me that a book might be of greater interest for a modern reader if the Squadron was recalled, not just as a small part at the sharp end, but as part of the vast effort made by the Royal Air Force to provide the United Kingdom with an organised fighter defence against enemy air attacks. As about fifty thousand RAF and WAAF personnel were employed on this work, many detailed books would be needed to do full justice to a subject about which the modern generation can scarcely have any knowledge, but about which I was able to learn quite a lot, and make my contribution between 1941 and 1945; and which I might be able to illustrate from my experience as Fighter Controller and as an Air Staff Officer.

In the context of this book it should, therefore, be emphasised that by the title "Fighters in Defence" I mean not only the fighter pilots but also a host of others including, for example, the staff officer groaning under the weight of the files in his in-tray, the engine fitter in the maintenance hanger, and the WAAF staring into a cathode ray tube on the Northumberland coast. There were so many others who do not even get a mention in these pages – thousands of them for whom I can but recall once more in the words of the famous RAF song:

"Bless 'em all, bless 'em all, the long and the short and the tall,
You'll get the promotion on this side of the ocean,
So cheer up my lads, bless 'em all.
(Nobody loves them, nobody cares, whether they're bald or covered with hairs.)"

The first chapter tells how I got hooked on flying and contains a brief description of the pre-war Auxiliary Air Force (the AAF) renamed the Royal Auxiliary Air Force (RAuxAF) in 1947. What follows is based mainly on my recollections of the men I knew and the events which took place nearly sixty years ago. I have striven for accuracy, but if I have gone off the rails I can only plead *anno domini*.

I have tried to avoid just another account of air battles, combats, victories and defeats, although some of that is needed to complete the picture. Books have already been written by or about outstanding pilots who served with the Squadron such as Paddy Finucane, Al Deere, Edward Howell, Sandy Johnstone, Ralph Sampson, Paddy Barthropp, Pierre Clostermann and others; but no account of 602 in the first defensive phase of the war would be complete without reference to our star turns, Archie McKellar, Findlay Boyd and Andrew McDowall, about whom I have written in the chapter about the Battle of Britain.

In the second chapter I learn to fly. The third chapter recalls some of the names and exploits of those who built up the Squadron before I joined in 1935. For this I have had to rely on the works of other authors to whom I am greatly indebted.

The fourth and fifth chapters give an idea of how the Squadron built itself up to meet the growing threat posed by Adolf Hitler. During this period the Squadron's addiction to rugby football dwindled, and any remaining semblance to a flying club gave way to increasing concern with tactical matters. The next two chapters continue this theme to the date of mobilisation, including a brief tribute to our regulars. The heading of the remaining chapters give sufficient clue to their contents.

I doubt if modern readers would thank me for swamping them with historical details and technical facts without reasons and comments required to understand their significance. I have gone, therefore, beyond the compass of the Squadron itself to describe briefly the function of the Fighter Command control and reporting system which enabled us to operate. In this connection it seemed appropriate to recall how the command of our forces was exercised with a chapter devoted to our Commander in Chief, Air Chief Marshal Lord Dowding of Bentley Priory, as seen from the Squadron level far below. Those serving at the heart and root of a military exercise such as the officers and airmen of a fighter squadron got a practical sight of the tree from the bottom upwards; but to complete the picture one needs to look down and outwards from the upper branches. That was not so easy in time of war when both strategy and tactics had to remain closely guarded secrets, covered by tight security. Fortunately these matters should now be an open book worth reading by those interested in the history of air warfare.

I never met "Stuffy", as our Commander in Chief was called, until long after the war. Since then I have, on several occasions, been called to pay tribute to his memory at the annual Remembrance Service in the place of his birth at Moffat. This has called for considerable enquiry and thought about him. As the history of the 20th century settles into prospective his strategic achievements will, I suspect, become increasingly significant. It may seem inopportune at this late date to dwell not only on his success but also on what, at the time, we regarded as tactical mistakes, such as the bullet grouping and the mis-harmonisation of our guns - also on the lack of armour plate behind the pilot's seat. I must, however, emphasise that we only saw these matters at the sharp end in the early months of the war without knowing the other considerations. Fortunately these things, which are further discussed in a later chapter, were put right before the real trouble started - not so the night flying situation for single seater day fighters in the early stages of the war which was, in fact, insoluble, but caused unnecessary wastage of aircraft and aircrew.

The fortunes of Fighter Command squadrons were dependent and closely linked with the control room reporting system (the C&R) which Lord Dowding helped to evolve during his time on the Staff at Air Ministry. I became part of this organisation as a Controller and Staff Officer during the later part of the war, so I am able to tell in outline how things developed on the ground and in the air as our defences developed.

As stated the organisation at its zenith deployed about fifty thousand men and women on the ground including my wife, Rachael M Hutchesson, who was initially employed as a plotter on the Command Operations table down the hole at Bentley Priory, after which she was commissioned into the Air Raid Warning Section. Then she became an Ops B Officer assistant to my duty controllers at the Group/Sector Operations Room situated in Stormont Building, Belfast.

The C & R system employed a number of auxiliary officers who had completed their tour of operations including Lloyd who had finished his tour with the Squadron before the war, Hosier Hodge, John Hawkes, Alastair Grant and Ian Ferguson, after his attachment as Personal Assistant to the Duke of Kent came to its sad end.

Although Fighter Command operations became increasingly offensive as the war developed the defensive role could never be relaxed in the United Kingdom until victory in Europe had been achieved. Moreover the British campaigns overseas called for continuous training of GCI and sector controllers and ground personnel for the necessary radar and operational control of fighters on offensive operations; not only to protect our forces in action and on the ground, but also to guard their establishments from enemy air attack. I have, therefore, drawn attention, not only to the system but the way we trained our personnel for it; not only in the busy sectors, but also during the long years in the dull inactive areas where German raids were few and far between, and where vigilance could never be relaxed.

The part played by the Squadron in the Second World War falls into two distinct phases. The defensive phase lasted from 3rd September 1939 to 7th June 1941 when the Squadron flew from Heathfield to Kenley. Till that date our role had been purely defensive after which 602 were mainly employed on offensive operations. Sweeps and attacks on special targets were made over France and the Low Countries; all aimed to tie down the Luftwaffe in the west and reduce the pressure on the Russians. Then came offensive operations in preparation for the Invasion of Europe.

So much has been said and written about the Battle of Britain that one tends to forget that Fighter Command were at it steadily for the whole war until 7th May 1945. 602 played a glorious part and suffered heavy casualties during this offensive phase which culminated in the support of the Army by cannon fire and bombs during the invasion and subsequent battles which lead to victory in Europe on 7th May 1945.

Fortunately the history of the offensive phase has been well recorded by authors such as Douglas MacRoberts and in books by some of the pilots themselves. They are all worth reading by those interested in the subject.

The offensive phase went on longer and took a heavier toll of causalities than suffered in defence during the earlier years of the war. I would like to have completed the brief chapter "In Memoriam" with a list of those who lost their lives after the Squadron went south in 1941, but have only been able to mention those I knew and remembered, and those listed in iThe Men of the Battle of Britain" by Kenneth G Wynn. Their achievements and those unlisted names are remembered with others in the RAF Memorial Window in Glasgow Cathedral, beside which hang the Squadron colours.

Students of air combat will not derive much inspiration from my personal experiences which only survived ten days of intensive operations and produced no more than about four shared victories during the earlier part of the war. However, there is plenty of combat detail published by Fighter Command authors including the books on 602. I have, therefore, confined myself to a few incidents still vivid in my memory.

Works of this kind inevitably focus on aircrew, almost to the exclusion of those officers and airmen on the ground without whom there would have been no flying. Being cursed by a complete failure to remember both names and faces, it is with shame that I can tell so little about our airmen who gave so much to the Squadron while we were getting ready for war, and then during the war years. Fortunately Dugald Cameron has been able to publish in the appendix to his book "Glasgow's Own" lists of all the auxiliary airmen who served with 602 up to 3rd September 1939, and then again the names of those who joined the post war Squadron during 1946 to 1957. Dugald was unable to produce such a list for the war years in the offensive stage owing to a lack of information. Some were posted in from other auxiliary squadrons but most would have been enlisted from the RAFVR.

With Dugald's approval I have annexed a copy of his Appendix giving the names of the squadron commanders, the pre war officers and the Battle of Britain pilots.

I have also added at the end an index of the names of most of those mentioned in these memoirs giving, where known, their ranks attained at the conclusion of their service. Where not known I have made a guess in the hope that I may be forgiven for any inaccuracies.

The Squadron was reformed at the Royal Naval Air Station, Abbotsinch, on 11th June 1946 under the command of Marcus Robinson, CB, AFC & Bar AE, DL, who nobly dropped from his war time rank of Group Captain to fill the established post of Squadron Leader. 602 were soon back in business under the command of five successive distinguished Commanding Officers. The first three were Auxiliaries and finally two were regulars.

The Squadron's contribution to our defences during 1947 to 1957 has been described in "Glasgow's Own" by Dugald Cameron. In retrospect I think the Air Council were right to disband not only the flying squadrons of the Auxiliary Air Force, but also the Fighter Control units including 3602 FCU to which I was appointed as the first Commanding Officer in 1948. The control system had become so secret and technical that it needed specialist regular personnel for its operation. Operational service flying had become highly professional and increasingly technical with costs to match measured in millions and even billions. Nevertheless the RAF were, in my view, over hasty in discarding an organisation ready made, not only for recruiting and training ground staff, but also for recruiting enthusiastic young civilians as officers and pilots in reserve for operational training to expand the service in the event of war and to replace causalities.

The Squadron's war record would not be complete without reference to the 602 Benevolent Fund founded by Sandy Johnstone and his brother officers, and taken under the wing of Glasgow's Lord Provost, Sir Patrick Dolan, an enthusiastic and loyal supporter of 602. The Fund has now been wholly expended by the Trustees in aid of many deserving cases. It was initially managed by Andrew Rintoul as Honorary Secretary and Treasurer, to be followed for many years by Hugh Glen Niven.

After 1957 the Squadron faded from memory till 1982 when Flight Lieutenant Bill McConnell of the RAFVR and his cadets of Number 2175 (Rolls Royce) Squadron of the Air Training Corps (ATC) dreamed up the idea of a museum to commemorate Glasgow's Squadron. An association was soon formed with the willing co-operation of the surviving members of the Squadron, most of whom became life members. The objects of the Association were to assist in the establishment and supervision of a museum to commemorate the Squadron and display its artifacts. The objects have been accomplished by Bill McConnell and his boys with the generous help of Rolls Royce, which shows what can be done with enthusiasm and leadership. The Museum is situated on the upper floor of a rifle range built by the Squadron on the ATC premises in Queen Elizabeth Road, Hillington behind the Rolls Royce factory. I have annexed a plan showing how to find the Museum by anyone contemplating a visit. The Museum has no income beyond occasional gifts and what can be raised by social functions. It is open during ATC training evenings.

The Museum owes much to the faithful efforts of Glen Niven who acted as Secretary of the Museum Association for fourteen years.

As a small contribution to the history of aviation in Scotland, and for the benefit of our family and his descendants, I have added a brief account of the early days of my uncle, Colonel A C H MacLean, CBE, one of the first pilots of the Royal Flying Corps (the RFC) who made a significant contribution to military flying during the six years following 1912, before returning to his regiment, The Royal Scots. A book could have been written about those six years in the life of Campbell MacLean but with the nonchalance and indifference of youth I never bothered to get the story out of him. My Uncle Campbell who rejoined the RAF as a pilot officer in 1940 qualifies for inclusion as a "Fighter in Defence".

For detail of some of the events at which I was not present I have relied heavily on "Lions Rampant" by Douglas MacRoberts, "Men of the Battle of Britain" by Kenneth G Wynn, "Glasgow's Own by Dugald Cameron and books by Sandy Johnstone.

Fortunately I was able to borrow from Donald Jack a copy of "Crying for the Moon" (a Former Wing Commander's memoirs of a vanished age) by William Matheson who was appointed our Assistant Adjutant in 1933. Fortunately Matheson, who had trained as a bomber pilot on Virginias, became an auxiliary enthusiast who seems to have enjoyed his time with the Squadron. By cribbing from his book I have been able to tell more about the years before I joined.

I am much indebted to my old Commanding Officer, Air Vice Marshal (Sandy) Johnstone CB, DFC, BE, and to my special friend, Wing Commander Donald Jack, for reading through the draft script to check the facts, and for his comments.

Without the inspiration of 602 Museum and the help of the Museum Association and Bill McConnell I would not have attempted these memoirs, some of which would have been lost.

CHAPTER 1
THE AUXILIARIES

In or about 1929 or 1930, among their efforts to prepare us for later life by learning something of public affairs, Canford School provided the Wimborne House common room with a number of suitable current publications. These included a well-known illustrated American magazine which published a picture and an article about one Adolf Hitler, a German, to whom I took an instant dislike. We had been brought up on the comforting belief that the Great War 1914/1918 had been the war to end wars. Here then was this evil looking person becoming famous in the land of our recent enemies by shouting and rioting in Munich beer cellars. God help us, I thought, if this fellow and his followers ever come to power in Germany. There could, and probably would be, another war. First impressions based merely on intuition can sometimes be right. This incidentally was just about the time the Labour government cancelled, ostensibly on medical grounds, the annual camps for public school Officers Training Corps held at the end of the summer term. Most people guessed it was really pacifism behind the decision. It was fine to get home for the holidays without having to sweat it out on Tidworth Pennings, but we were old enough to recognise the short sighted hypocrisy which was to prove so dangerous and misleading in later years.

In the early thirties before starting on my Law Degree at Glasgow University I joined a small party led by my friend, George Coulson, a fluent German speaker. We walked round lovely Schleisvig Holstein, sleeping on incredibly hard steel wire mattresses in the German youth hostels - no doubt designed to toughen the young master race who were already much in evidence in their brown shirts and swastika arm bands marching round the streets like soldiers - and enjoying it.

Although Hitler was not yet Chancellor his influence was everywhere. To those on the spot it looked like a foregone conclusion, but apparently not so recognised in Britain.

Professor Max Goose, a Hamburg school master, and his family with whom we stayed, clearly disliked the way things were going; but by then it was obviously too late and potentially dangerous for ordinary thinking people to do much more than watch with dismay the course events were taking. When asked how I thought the younger members of their large family were coming on, to their distress, and with the youthful lack of tact, "Very well" I replied, "but they can scarcely avoid becoming young Nazis in due course." Feeling increasingly uncomfortable and out of place in this distasteful environment, and to George's disappointment, I cut short my first and last visit to the Reich. Looking back my youthful reaction was understandable, but in retrospect regrettable.

During my first year at Glasgow University the students at Oxford and Cambridge and other English seats of learning voted in favour of a resolution that they would not serve their King and country in the armed forces in an event of an emergency. Randolph Churchill led the opposition to these resolutions, but they paid him little heed. In due course a hastily badly publicised impromptu debate took place in the Glasgow male students union during the lunch hour. To my disgust the students who bothered to attend went the same way as their English counterparts by a large majority. Fortunately such students were in no position to influence events, but their resolutions must have given great comfort to Adolf Hitler who had already written a book, which nobody had bothered to read, explaining just what he was going to do and what he did do. There was, in fact, nothing weak and rotten about our students, but I am certain that was the impression they made on the Nazis who tended to believe what they wanted to believe.

Against this background I heard of the Auxiliary Air Force from a more senior student, one Edward Howell, with whom I sometimes sat at lunch in the union. Here indeed was a way to prepare for Hitler and at the same time learn to fly an aeroplane. I had always had a secret plan to own my own aeroplane one day when I could afford it. It was an ambition I never achieved.

In 1933 I duly presented myself to Flight Lieutenant George Stacey Hodson

The Marquess of Douglas and Clydesdale AFC
Commanding Officer 602 Squadron
May 1932 – September 1936

AFC, the Adjutant of 602 Squadron at Renfrew and was interviewed by Lord Clydesdale, the Commanding Officer. Hoddy was detailed to give me a ride in a Wapiti in which he performed the usual aerobatics. I enjoyed the experience with the possible exception of the slow roll during which the startled passenger finds himself upside down, hanging in the straps. The roll is an exhilarating experience for the pilot, but over-rated as a joy in the back seat.

The C.O. seemed reasonably encouraging, but when the full training commitment was explained I realised that I simply could not cope with the Squadron during the second and third years of my Degree Course, coupled with full time apprenticeship in a legal office. Clydesdale understood the situation and agreed to reconsider me after graduation.

In November 1935 I graduated as a Bachelor of Law by which time I had renewed my application to join 602 and had been accepted subject to medical examination by Doc Allan. He could find nothing wrong with me.

At this point it seems appropriate to tell a bit more about the Auxiliaries.

Although much has been written about the Auxiliary Air Force (AAF), renamed the Royal Auxiliary Air Force (RAuxAF) in 1947, I have rarely met anyone under the age of sixty who ever heard of it. In order to understand what follows a brief description of the purpose and constitution of the AAF should be helpful to a reader with little knowledge of aviation history.

When the AAF is mentioned people often ask, "Were those the University Air Squadrons or were they the Royal Air Force Volunteer Reserve (RAFVR)?" Both of these were quite different in concept from the Auxiliary Air Force being concerned with the training of individuals; the former providing elementary flying training instruction and experience for University students, and the latter for individual flying training to Service standards. By contrast the Auxiliary Air Force was raised to produce squadrons for the RAF, creating and maintaining not just a reserve, but a complete fighting unit equivalent to the Territorial Battalions of the Army. The Squadrons were designed to train not only aircrew but also ground crew for all trades ready for immediate mobilisation. Because of the technical nature of the aircraft maintenance, and the need to keep in flying practice for safety, the training commitment was inevitably heavier than for the Territorial Army. Three weekends per month and two evenings a week were expected.

The Flying Squadrons of the Auxiliary Air Force came into existence in 1925 on the initiative of Marshal of the Royal Air Force, Lord Trenchard. The original squadrons were numbered 600 to 608, but 606 was tactfully omitted because it was, at that time, the official medicine approved for the treatment of syphilis!

The squadrons were named after and located near to centres of population from which they recruited their members. They were as follows:

SQUADRON NUMBER	DATE FORMED	PEACETIME BASE
*602 (City of Glasgow) Squadron	12 Sep.1925	Renfrew/Abbotsinch
*600 (City of London) Squadron	14 Oct.1925	Hendon
*601 (County of London) Squadron	14 Oct.1925	Hendon
*603 (City of Edinburgh) Squadron	14 Oct.1925	Turnhouse
*605 (County of Warwick) Squadron	5 Oct.1926	Castle Bromwich
*604 (County of Middlesex) Squadron	17 Mar.1930	Hendon
*607 (County of Durham) Squadron	17 Mar.1930	Usworth
608 (North Riding) Squadron	17 Mar.1930	Thornaby
*609 (West Riding of Yorkshire) Squadron	10 Feb.1936	Yeadon
*610 (County of Chester) Squadron	10 Feb.1936	Hooten Park
*611 (West Lancashire) Squadron	10 Feb.1936	Speke
612 (County of Aberdeen) Squadron	1 Jun.1937	Dyce
614 (County of Glamorgan) Squadron	1 Jun.1937	Llandow
*615 (County of Surrey) Squadron	1 Jun.1937	Kenley
*616 (South Yorkshire) Squadron	1 Nov.1938	Leconfield
613 (City of Manchester) Squadron	1 Mar.1939	Ringway

Special Reserve Squadrons incorporated into the Auxiliary Air Force at later dates:

503 (County of Lincoln) Squadron	5 Oct.1926	Waddington
*504 (County of Nottingham) Squadron	26 Mar.1928	Hucknall
*501 (County of Gloucester) Squadron	14 Jun.1929	Filton
500 (County of Kent) Squadron	16 Mar.1931	Manston
502 (County of Ulster) Squadron	15 May.1925	Aldergrove

———————

21 Squadrons

When the Auxiliary Squadrons were mobilised on 14th August 1939 about forty per cent of the pilot strength of Fighter Command were auxiliaries. Their story has been written by Leslie Hunt in his book – "Twenty one Squadrons" published in 1972 by Garnstone Press Ltd.

The fourteen Squadrons marked with an asterisk formed nearly a quarter of the Fighter Command Order of Battle on 7th September 1940. The remaining seven Squadrons of the Auxiliary Air Force were employed in other commands.

Apart from the noise of Rolls Royce Kestrel engines over Paisley on Saturdays and Sundays, the Squadron's activities were relatively unknown in Glasgow. This was brought home to me by an amusing incident which took place during a church parade held in 1938 on a Sunday afternoon in the St Andrews Hall where we joined the RNVR and the Territorial Army. After the service the whole parade was drawn up outside the hall prior to marching up Bath Street and past the saluting base outside the Royal Scottish Automobile Club in Blythswood Square. While waiting for the order to march two wee lads came running down the lines. The elder boy was clearly a military enthusiast. We heard him yell to his wee brother "Yon's the H.L.I. and there's the Navy". They paused for breath. "Whit are they"? shouted the wee chap pointing to the Squadron. The elder boy hesitated but soon had the answer. "Ach they're the Germans" he shouted. Our troops were convulsed, I think it made their day.

Marching up Bath Street with Douglas Farquhar leading we attracted the attention of a drunk man who was making a scene dancing and shouting on the pavement. He fell in at the front marching beside Douglas, cavorting, and mocking our progress. The C.O. got his measure. He gave a light push to the man's shoulder just as he was off balance on one foot. Our tormentor reeled and fell among the crowd on the pavement. It was very neatly done, and side stepped a situation which might have got out of control. It was a typical reaction by Douglas who was never afraid of taking a risk.

In peacetime 602 was hard work; but fun because all ranks including the commanding officers, our regulars and our airmen were blessed with that curious sense of humour which pervades the RAF, and which combined well with the Glaswegian brand. We all took the business quite seriously but with a light touch. Discipline was adequate and founded on enthusiasm. RAF bull was accepted as inevitable. 'Bullshit pays' was the sarcastic slogan in use.

CHAPTER 2
AIR BORN

Findlay Boyd and I were new boys in November 1935. Findlay had been well advised to get his 'A' Licence with the Scottish Flying Club because he was soon tested by Mark Selway and commissioned. I did not fare so well having to hang about for several months waiting for the services of an available instructor who could find time to deal with me.

Later in 1936 we were joined by Ian Ferguson who did his training with the Squadron. He and Findlay were assigned to join George Pinkerton and Sandy Johnstone in B Flight under John Feather.

In 1935 the squadron fielded nine operational Hawker Harts in three flights – A Flight under David McIntyre AFC, B Flight under John Feather and C Flight in charge of Andrew Douglas Farquhar. In addition to the dual Hart trainer we had about three Avro 504s. These

Avro 504N, K1982 at Abbotsinch

were yellow bi-planes of antique aspect powered by an uncowled radial Lynx engine. The 504 had been in service as a trainer since 1916 when my uncle, Campbell MacLean, was equipped with them during his command of the Central Flying School at the Royal Flying Corps (RFC), which gives an indication of the priority and the money devoted by the RAF to initial flying training between the wars. The Avro must have been the first step on the ladder for hundreds, it not thousands, of service pilots. The cruising speed of 70 mph was low, nor could the Avro climb to a great height. The cockpit was so pure and cold at 7,000 ft that it was reputed to kill off any cold germs that might be brewing up. Indeed I tried it on one occasion and it seemed to work!

In or about 1932 the Wapiti had been superseded by the Hawker Hart light bomber. These were a joy to fly but not such a joy for the bomb aimer lying on the floor in the back.

It was rather depressing to realise that this delightful little aeroplane was the standard bombing equipment of the RAF, while Pathe News Gazettes in the cinemas were showing American civilian passengers riding around the United States in Douglas DC2 airliners which could cruise above our top speed.

I first took to the air on 17th November 1935 in an Avro 504 with David McIntyre as my instructor. None of those I encountered could match his calm and courteous handling of a pupil.

As the result of my spasmodic and spread out training I only went solo on 15th March 1936 after eleven hours dual, and was thereafter commissioned in the exalted rank of Pilot Officer, to become a Bomber Pilot who never dropped a bomb!

Earlier in 1935 the Squadron had, during summer camp, won a prize for their bombing with better results than any other squadron in the whole of the RAF. That was certainly an

Squadron Leader D F McIntyre AFC
Commanding Officer 602 Squadron
September 1936 – October 1937

achievement for a bunch of amateurs, particularly for our bomb aimers, proving what could be done with enthusiasm and hard work. It also caused a reappraisal of the Auxiliary Air orce which was thereafter considered part of the RAF front line.

Despite the Squadron's record I was never impressed by our high level bombing system, nor with the primitive and extremely uncomfortable bomb aiming equipment fitted to our Hawker Hinds. The most satisfactory feature of our bomber role was the opportunity of getting our auxiliary airmen into the air, which sadly came to an end when we converted to single seater fighters.

Despite the weakness of the precision bombing system, when it came to dive bombing we were dab hands. This took the form of vertical dives from a stall turn at about 10,000 feet. The Hind with all its wires and struts reached its terminal velocity at about 340 miles per hour, at which point the pilot released his bag of flour and put his trust in God and his flying wires to get him out of the dive in time - good fun which I hope my air gunners, Parnie and Conway, enjoyed. The results were really quite accurate which were borne out later by the performance of the German Stukas. It is a pity the Royal Air Force and, especially the Royal navy, did not take dive bombing more seriously before we went to war. The evidence was there.

Soon after my solo flight Mark despatched me on my first cross country to Turnhouse with strict instructions to report my advent to the duty pilot as required by the rules. I went off in my Avro 504. With its cruising speed of about 70 miles per hour and a following wind I soon covered the 50 odd miles and made a poor landing at Turnhouse which ended up with a swing to starboard, followed by a ground loop with the aeroplane facing the way it came! At this point I began to realise the significance of the bamboo hoops fitted under the ends of each lower wing tip. In shame I taxied up to hanger hoping that no one had been watching. Alighting from the Avro I approached a group of rather languid looking young men in flying overalls. Either they had not seen the landing or were too polite to comment.

I announced my arrival from Abbotsinch, but the news made little impression on these representatives of 603 City of Edinburgh Squadron. I tried again - could they direct me to the Duty Pilot? But this overture was greeted with blank stares.

"I have been ordered to report to the Duty Pilot - where is he?" Suddenly a gleam of recognition flashed across one of the faces, "He's flying" he replied. I sensed that he was too polite to add the words ìof courseî for the benefit of uninitiated. I gave up. "Tell him that Pilot Officer MacLean was here and is now returning to Abbotsinch". This they agreed to do. My prop was still turning so off I went. Such was my first encounter with our redoubtable Edinburgh rivals. On my return I told Mark about the landing. "What did you do when the swerve to starboard began and the wing dropped?" "Port rudder" I said. "Quite wrong" replied Mark. "If you had applied hard starboard rudder when the swerve began the aircraft would have heeled over to port and it would have straightened up". Who would have thought of it except Isaac Newton! It happened to me once more and Mark's remedy worked like a charm.

On 7th June 1936 Mark decided I needed further instruction. On take off, to my surprise and horror, at 300 feet there was a loud bang from the radial engine which had lost two of its push rods and all of its power. The stick was wrenched out of my hands by Mark and slammed against the dashboard with such force that I nearly lost my fingers - but better than losing our lives in a take off stall. Down swooped Mark, and with a violent crab side slip over a hedge we alighted in a tiny triangular meadow full of cows. I never realised the enormous curiosity which haunts the cow. This herd were obviously intrigued by a such a large yellow string bag apparition. Perhaps they mistook the Avro for a splendid new bull dropped in from heaven because I spent the next twenty minutes fending them off. No sooner would I shoo them away from the prop then the others would be nibbling the tail plane. I was glad to be relieved of these agricultural duties when Mark returned with the rescue crew from Abbotsinch.

With only thirteen hours solo in my log book these memoirs nearly did not get written so you may be reading by the courtesy of the late Air Marshal Sir Anthony Dunmore Selway - one life gone!

Annual training in 1936 took place at Tangmere in Sussex. Clydesdale very decently tossed up with his Flight Commanders for the laborious chore of leading the Avros to Tangmere. He lost the toss, so on 10th July 1936 we took off on the first leg to Yeadon. The flight lasted 2 hours 55 minutes under lowering clouds across the Southern Uplands and the Pennines. 609 West Riding Squadron were just forming at Yeadon. We had lunch with Beaumont and Pip Barron and would see more of them at Drem during the war. The second leg to Upper Heyford took 1 hour 55 minutes. Then on we flew to Tangmere, a rapid flight of 1 hour and 15 minutes.

The Avro had a comparatively low ceiling above which it could not climb although 17,000 ft was achieved. There was no external means of fixing one's position so we flew on a compass course making due allowance for cross winds to achieve the desired track across the map. If things got really difficult one could follow a railway or a canal. It was not advisable to climb up above the clouds to do the trip on a compass course with the prospect of coming down blind through ten tenths cloud and perhaps hitting a hill or an electricity grid; as Findlay Boyd did on one occasion, cutting off all the power in Kilmarnock.

The Squadron aircraft were not fitted with RT (radio telephone) until 1939. Although much of our flying was done above and through the clouds one always had to bear in mind what went up had to come down. Scotland, with its unpredictable weather and hills all over the map, tended to make us rather more careful than our English counterparts.

At my first camp I converted to Hawker Hinds under the guidance of the C.O. who had recently qualified as an instructor. After 45 minutes he grew weary of the operation and I was turned loose on my first service type. I was just in time because the phone rang and my instructor was summoned by the Whips to drop it all and attend a debate in the House of Commons.

At Tangmere R Musprat Williams and I were about the same vintage as aspiring pilots. Sprat as he was known was a very unusual man - almost an enigma. No doubt due to his enormous personal charm Sprat was employed as Secretary to the C.Os father, the Duke of Hamilton. As a result he was duly recruited as an officer in 602 together with E V N Bell. Sprat made many aristocratic friends, and was a welcome guest at several noble establishments. His "castle creeping" became the subject of much leg pulling which he bore with good grace.

Sprat was always accompanied by Mickey Mouse, a cross between a wolf and a husky, with an unpredictable and potentially ferocious temperament. According to Sprat while he was in China Mickey attached and castrated a prowling Chinaman after which it was decided that his master should leave that country without delay. Accordingly Sprat and Mickey boarded the Trans Siberian express armed with a Primus stove and a packet of sausages. They were duly allotted space in an empty van. Sprat lit his stove and began to cook his sausages. Suddenly there was a huge jolt as the train ran into a snowdrift. The stove and sausages went on fire and destroyed the van. Musprat Williams was clearly a saboteur. He was arrested and condemned to death by the local Soviet. Fortunately the news got out before it was too late, and with the help of influence he was allowed to return to Britain.

Our return from Tangmere on 1st August 1936 was a dicey affair. The Avros led by Flying Officer McIntrye, the assistant adjutant, took off for Hendon at about 8.45 a.m. We were soon down to ground level under low cloud, scraping over the top of the Downs, flying so low that I had to swerve to clear a hay stack on top of a ridge. McIntyre, who was noted for his navigation, had had enough and wisely turned back to Tangmere where we landed a full hour after take off. Just before 1.00 p.m. we managed to snake our way under clouds to Hendon. It had been quite an experience for beginners. Camp was over so we were ordered home by train.

The Hinds could not do much better. They scraped into Hendon. London drew them like a magnet. After a good lunch some of them were reported to have visited Green Park tube station attempting to dash to the top of the down going moving staircase. Only one is said to have made it but he threw up at the top! A more restrained party accompanied Sprat for a Turkish bath. I cannot remember how the Hinds and their crews got home.

When the Squadron resumed training in September 1936 I took an unpleasant jolt. Mark, who cannot have been paying much attention to the weather, told me to do a trip in a Hind round the Clyde coast at 4,000 feet. As soon as I reached height over Bishopton I ran into cloud. The instruments were still a mystery so I just ploughed on as ordered. At the end of two minutes which defy description I emerged in a vertical dive pulling out just in time to avoid the cranes in Lithgowís shipbuilding yard. Something would have to be done about those instruments!

My next jolt was more serious. Mark decided I was fit for a longer cross country flight and despatched me to Speke aerodrome near Liverpool. Flying control at Abbotsinch was almost non existent, but Speke turned out to be very avant-guard complete with a control tower and a duty pilot armed with red and green lights - something I had not yet encountered. Both colours were flashing so I foolishly decided to land. Unfortunately the red was for me and the green for someone else! While landing we missed each other by a hairs breadth. The other pilot did not like it neither did the duty pilot. A report was made and I had to fly back to Speke to face a formal enquiry. The proceedings were solemn and conducted with courtesy by a Squadron Leader of Great War vintage. I escaped with a telling off which was better than a Court Martial. I was lucky. It had been my second brush with the Reaper. Who was I to poke fun at 603 about their sketchy flying control arrangements at Turnhouse!

CHAPTER 3
EARLY BIRDS

Service in the Auxiliary Air Force could be extended but normally came to an end in five years. Those who could have told about the officers and airmen who served during the ten years before I joined are mainly deceased or have disappeared. To our comrades now gone and to those still with us we can only say "Thank You".

When I joined in 1935, Squadron Leader, the Marquis of Douglas and Clydesdale AFC (known to his friends as Douglo) had been in the command for several years, during which time he had also sat as a Member of Parliament for a Renfrewshire constituency. He was also Acting Station Commander of RAF Station Abbotsinch, a task which mainly devolved on the shoulders of his regular adjutant. This was, indeed, an odd situation whereby an Auxiliary Officer (presumably unpaid) was in command of an RAF station. Under his courteous and charming manner beat a heart of a lion; not only demonstrated by his flying, but as an amateur champion class middle weight boxer. Douglo and his three brothers, Geordie, CO of 603 Squadron in Edinburgh, Lord Malcolm Douglas Hamilton and Lord David Douglas Hamilton were all pilots. Clydesdale's initiative in promoting the flights over Mount Everest and his courage in executing that hazardous enterprise together with his Flight Commander, David McIntyre, the other pilot of the Expedition, had made him a legendary figure in his generation. Reading their account of that perilous escapade in the Pilot's Book of Everest, one recognises the professional performance of those two amateurs operating at the extreme limits of their aircraft and equipment.

Despite his undoubted ability Douglo was rather vague and poor on detail. He was fortunate in having appointed as his Secretary E V N Bell, an ex Guards Officer, who was scrupulously efficient in those qualities lacked by his chief. As a sitting M.P. we did not see as much of the CO as we would have liked. He would fly over to Abbotsinch from a field near Dungavel at Strathaven in his own light monoplane. This aeroplane brings back an interesting memory of my first camp at Tangmere when he invited me to fly with him to an aerodrome somewhere south east of London where they were building him a new aircraft - a Miles Vega I seem to remember. It looked like rain so I stuffed my service raincoat into the aeroplane locker and promptly forgot about it. Later in August my mother asked what I had done with my raincoat. "Good heavens Ma" I said "its probably gone with the CO and the British Olympic Team to the Munich Games". Indeed it had. When next he came to Abbotsinch and I retrieved my coat which had remained unnoticed for two months. On that occasion our CO who attended a formal reception given by Hess must have made a great impression on his German hosts; which was to be the cause of trouble and embarrassment for him at a later date.

Apart from the Squadron Clydesdale and McIntyre were closely involved with Scottish aviation in the foundation of Prestwick. I wish I could write in more detail about Clydesdale's contribution. Prestwick was, and still is, a wonderful enterprise which has never been fully developed as it should have been. They also built Grangemouth Airfield which was Mac's dream of a central airport for Scotland for which it would have been ideal. It was to become a petrochemical complex.

By good fortune Donald Jack has been in touch with Wing Commander William Robert Matheson who recently published an autobiography of the first twenty-five years of his life, coming to an end with two years spent as Assistant Adjutant of 602 at Abbotsinch.

At that stage Matheson, an experienced bomber pilot on Vickers Virginias, was not yet an instructor. On reporting for duty Flight Lieutenant Hodson could not promise him much flying, but made Matheson responsible for ground lectures and, what is more important, getting the "blighters to turn up". "You will also", he said "be Officer in Charge of the Fire Fighting Section, the Armoury, the Photographic and the Parachute sections, the Sergeants Mess, the Service Institute, the Orderly Room and keeping an eye on the officers mess!" "Surely that is for the PMC" remarked Matheson. "I know" said Hoddy "but remember these chaps have volunteered to fly, and it is a hell of a job to get them to do any ground work". Bill Matheson tottered from the presence, but to his surprise mastered all these tasks with the help of his excellent regular NCOs.

Soon after his arrival the new Assistant Adjutant was introduced to his Commanding Officer who had just returned from the Himalayas. He liked the way the CO looked directly at him and his friendly smile.

In July 1933 the Squadron consisting of ten Wapitis took off in three flights, bound for Hawkinge. To the surprise of the Assistant Adjutant, after about fifteen minutes the CO suddenly disappeared and his place was taken by the Senior Flight Commander - McIntyre, no doubt. The matter became the subject for discussion in the mess at Hawkinge. Matheson recalls the conversation. Perhaps he had remembered some urgent unfinished parliamentary work and had gone back to complete it. One of the junior officers ventured the suggestion that the C.O. with all his pressing responsibilities had absent mindedly over looked the fact that he was leading the Squadron. It was just decided to disagree and the matter was left at that. Clydesdale arrived at Hawkinge the next day.

Matheson was due to represent the RAF in a boxing competition. The Boxing Marquis apparently took the matter to heart, and was in the habit of rousting his Assistant Adjutant from his bed for a cross country run before breakfast at camp to keep him fit for the event.

One foggy morning at Hawkinge the Padre, Louis Sutherland, thumbed a ride in a Wapiti with Matheson who warned him he was risking his life in such poor visibility. "In that case, dear boy" replied the padre "you have a damn sight better chance of entering the Heavenly Realm with me on board!"

Shortly after the Hawkinge camp Clydesdale asked Matheson if he would bring his private aeroplane from Abbotsinch to his private landing field at Dungavel near Strathaven. Although he had not flown the aeroplane before he was in little doubt he could handle this short flight; but when he saw Dungavel he realised he could be in trouble. It looked no bigger than a pocket-handkerchief, surrounded by fir trees with a nasty cross wind blowing. He came in diagonally to offset the cross wind and clear the trees but landed too fast. Unfortunately there was a deep gully near the boundary into which the little high wing monoplane went on its nose; and there soon arrived the Marquis dressed in a smart suit already to go. Matheson must have been in despair, but the CO just said "Hard luck, I nearly did it myself once. I shall have to get that ditch marked". Later he gave his unfortunate Assistant Adjutant the boss of the broken airscrew which he shaped into a clock! Matheson had liked his Commanding Officer very much before this incident, but in his words "from that moment I loved him".

It is interesting to note that this pocket handkerchief was the airfield Hess, the Deputy Fuhrer, had planned to land his Me110 in 1941. Just as well he never found it, or perhaps it would have saved him many years of misery if he had!

In September 1933 the Air Ministry ordered the Squadron to "attack" the fleet concentrated at May Island in the Firth of Forth as part of a combined RAF and Naval exercise. Two bombing attacks were made by the Wapitis who were credited with the sinking of one battleship for the loss of one aircraft – shades of things to come in 1942 at Kota Baru, Malaya.

Although above average on Virginias Bill Matheson had his ups and downs. With several auxiliaries clamouring to be airborne Hoddy sent him off in a Wapiti to do a weather test. Conditions were worse than expected so in he came searching anxiously for the aerodrome boundary. Too late - the leading edge of his starboard main plane scraped through the branches of a tree, somersaulting the Wapiti with its pilot and passenger on to its nose. Wisely he switched off the petrol and ignition, but blood was pouring over his overalls. "To hell with it" muttered Matheson, "I've broken by bloody arm". At which came a voice from behind "No you haven't Sir, you have broken my bloody nose". "Do I get a wound stripe" asked the disconsolate air gunner when they reached sick quarters. The remains of the tree became known as "Matheson's Folly". It was probably bulldozed away when Abbotsinch was extended.

The Assistant Adjutant's lectures were the best thing he could do to brighten the lives of the frustrated pilots grounded by filthy Scottish weather. After rather a splendid Squadron formation the pilots were getting out of their flying overalls in the crew room. Matheson offered his congratulations. "Thank you dear boy" said one. "It was better than listening to your lectures". "You never come to them replied Matheson". "I know" replied the pilot, "but I have heard about them". In spite of that the Assistant Adjutant had to admit the incredible. Those who never came always seemed to get the best exam results. He might just as well have been on leave! He was, however, invited by two of the wilder junior officers to join them in a treasure hunt, but was advised against it by one of the Flight Commanders. On a previous occasion there had been a near scandal resulting in letters of apology having to be sent out. The treasure hunt had been a success, except that one young officer had managed to intercept a pair of the Lord Provost's pants en route to the cleaners! This had been leaked to the press and had caused the Squadron considerable embarrassment. The Assistant Adjutant as a regular did not wish to be involved in such dare devilry. "Who knows", he thought, "someone might purloin the Stone of Destiny and create a national crisis".

In February 1934 the Squadron was re-equipped with the Hawker Hart, the RAF standard light bomber with a 600 horse power Rolls Royce Kestrel engine, giving it a cruising speed of 130 miles per hour and a top speed of about 170 miles per hour. The boys were clamouring to fly it, but there was a slight problem. The Hart just loved flying. It was supposed to stall at 58 miles per hour, but unless one settled smoothly down on the ground, kissing the turf in a three point landing, the aeroplane would spring again into the air and proceed across the aerodrome in a series of hops and bumps, greeted by the ground staff with hoots of derision.

Hawker Harts, K3054, K1420 & K3870 at Abbotsinch

It was soon the turn of the Assistant Adjutant. Being experienced in sedate aeroplanes such as Virginias and Wapitis he made sure there were no auxiliary witnesses on the touch line. Sure enough he bounded nearly 50 feet into the air. "Thank God one of those young fellows didn't see it", said Hoddy. Despite that the CO still had great confidence in Flying Officer Matheson as a pilot and entrusted him with the life of his private secretary, Flying Officer Vivian Bell, as a passenger on a flight to Hendon. He had previously received from Ding Dong a snapshot of the CO's aeroplane on its nose with Clydesdale pointing at it and with a caption written underneath "Uncle is very annoyed with you". Matheson decided to get his own back. As they were crossing the border a nonchalant voice through the speaking tube announced, "Oh by the way, I'm going to try and land you at Dungavel. It will get you back sooner." One word only came back through the intercom. "Christ". "Were you talking to me?" enquired Matheson. "No, to the Almighty" said Ding Dong. "Nobody has ever landed a Hart there before". "That's all right" replied the pilot, "There's always a first time". "It will be the last time" was Ding Dong's comment. He must have heaved a sigh of relief as they passed safely by Strathaven to land at Abbotsinch.

Our aerodrome could be very exposed to gales as Ding Dong was to discover when he took off into a strong wind which increased to gale force while he was air borne. Would he be the only man in the air force to land a Hart backwards? The penny dropped on the ground, and out went the gallant airmen who snatched down the wings while Ding Dong's aircraft, with an air speed of about equal to the speed of the wind, hovered almost stationery above them. They lowered him down to safety. He fared better than the unfortunate Alastair Grant in an Avro who had just made a successful landing at camp, and was blown backwards upside down.

There was another little pitfall in waiting for the Hart pilot who was supposed to take off on the gravity tank situated in the centre section of the upper wing, and which was fitted with a lever underneath to switch over to the main tank. With a slip stream of 140 miles per hour it was advisable to stream line the hand before reaching up to this lever and avoid having ones arm violently blown backwards. During the camp at Lympne in 1934 Edward Howell overlooked this little formality, and began to enjoy some low flying over south London. Sure enough his engine suddenly spluttered and died; but his luck was in, there was a tree lined lane ahead which enabled him to land in the forbidden precincts of Windsor Great Park. In the days of good Kings James, the sponsor of the authorised version of the Bible, Howell would have been executed. It was the capital offence to bring armed weapons into the Park. However, the guards officers on the spot failed even to place him under arrest, but gave him an excellent lunch and waved him off with a very red face to Lympne with the aid of his main tank! The CO was not amused. Overdue action was in force. The RAF were searching the English Channel for Edward's remains. Of course, the press got hold of the story and some rude fellows suggested that a Pimms party had produced partial paralysis. Air Commodore Baldwin AOC No 6 Auxiliary Group arrived at Lympne to deliver his rocket. Baldwin was blessed with a sense of humour so, with the aid of a few Mess Pimms, the AOC was persuaded to return to Group without doing too much damage.

Early in 1935 Flight Lieutenant Anthony (known as "Mark") Dunmore Selway took over as regular Adjutant from Hoddy. Flying Officer McIntyre was appointed as his Assistant Adjutant.

Fortunately for posterity the first forty pages of Douglas McRobert's book contain more of the early history of the Squadron before I joined it in November 1935. Before passing on beyond that date I cannot resist retelling the tale of the Royal Review in 1935 at Mildenhall where the Squadron was represented by three Harts in charge of Douglas Farquhar, Andrew Rintoul and the new Adjutant Mark Selway. There being no station accommodation for such a large gathering the auxiliary pilots were banished under canvas and were even refused

RAF Abbotsinch in the mid-1930s

access to the officers' mess. In the local hotel the 602 men hatched their plot. If they could not get in those inside the mess were not going to get out. At about 2.00 a.m. they helped themselves to some convenient adjacent building supplies, and then creeping up to the mess, and under the noise cover from the snoring occupants, they proceeded to brick up all the entrances. These remained well and truly blocked when His Majesty arrived the next morning. Mildenhall may have learned some manners. Nothing was said. One can but admire Mark Selway who must have put his regular career at risk.

Before I joined a number of the older pilots had completed their service with the

Squadron including Flight Lieutenant Lennox, succeeded as Flight Commander by John Feather, also David Lloyd a steelmaker who became a Fighter Controller, Maurice Renshaw, and T A B Smith, a scientific instrument maker who designed our bomb sight - and Donald Law who took command in 1939 of No.20 Squadron based in India.

In peace time opportunities for promotion in the Auxiliary Air Force were rare and far between. By 1935 Dennis McNab, a qualified instructor, and John Feather were nearing the end of their time. During the war their experience and skill made a vital contribution to teaching young pilots to fly. Those who had resigned or completed their service included, Edward Howell commissioned in the RAF as a Regular Officer, Maurice Renshaw and John Shewell. Andrew Rintoul, a busy Chartered Accountant, extended his commission and on mobilisation was employed in the accountancy branch where he rose to the rank of Wing Commander.

George Pinkerton and Marcus Robinson were Senior Flying Officers, both experienced and proficient in the air and on the ground. After these came Sandy Johnstone, Dunlop Urie, John Hawkes and Alastair Grant.

Quite a lot has been said and written about George Pinkerton who enjoyed, or perhaps more accurately, suffered, a good deal of publicity as a result of the part he played in the Battle of the Forth. He served briefly in command of 65 Squadron before his return to 602 in April 1940. George was raised and trained in the family market garden business which specialised in growing rhubarb. He did not like eating the stuff himself, but soon developed a successful branch of the business near Houston. As a young man seeking adventure he acquired a motor bicycle, and got so keen that he volunteered to ride for a Wall of Death in a showground. This landed him in hospital. Presumably he then decided that flying would be a safer bet, and joined the Scottish Flying Club at Renfrew. This, of course, led him towards 602 where he could pursue his hobby at considerably lower cost!

Shortly before the outbreak of war George the Senior Flying Officer took over B Flight from John Feather. He was brought back in March or April 1940 to succeed Douglas Farquhar in command of 602.

George was, I think, what the country people of Scotland used to call "A wide man", a shrewd down-to-earth judge of men and business matters coupled with a whole range of practical skills. After the war he returned to farming, but also found the energy and ability to serve as a County Councillor, a Commissioner for Income Tax and as a JP He also found time to do case work for the RAF Benevolent Fund. His appointment as a Deputy Lieutenant of the County of Renfrew was most appropriate.

D F McIntyre, of whom more later, was appointed Commanding Officer of the Squadron towards the end of 1936. He was succeeded in 'A' Flight by Marcus Robinson. Like myself Marcus was born in the West End of Glasgow. According to my mother Marcus was wheeled in a splendid perambulator envied and admired by my father's sisters. To my Mother's irritation they would draw attention to the Robinson model and compare it with the inferior MacLean chariot. With such a start Marcus could scarcely go wrong, and so on to Warristan in Moffat, a rival preparatory school of St Ninians, which was later to have the doubtful pleasure of my company. Even at this tender age young Robinson was beginning to show signs of a stubborn, unyielding nature, with his hands firmly entrenched in his trouser pockets despite all cautions and warnings against the practise. However, he soon met his match in the shape of the headmaster's wife, Mrs Gardiner. Rising from his bed young Robinson donned his shorts and reached down happily for his pockets; but they had gone. The matron had sewed them up! After Warristan he completed his education at Rossal; and then he joined the family timber business. By 1935 Marcus was already a polished pilot, almost as good in the air as he was at ballroom dancing, for which he was nicknamed at the time as "Slipstream". As a Flight Commander he proved a success - courteous but strict on the ground, and great fun in the Mess. Early in 1940 Marcus was appointed to command 616 South Yorkshire Auxiliary Squadron at Leconfield. He led them over Dunkirk and into the Battle of Britain.

On transfer to Training Command, Robinson became a rapid success rising steadily to the rank of Acting Group Captain in command of RAF Church Lawford. His unorthodox approach to flying training seems to have paid off because he was awarded the Air Force Cross and a Bar to that medal for his efforts. Marcus would personally check the performance of his instructors. One of his little ploys was to fit a duplicate hidden set of engine switches near his seat in his Oxford. Suddenly there would be engine failure. On the conclusion of the test he would switch on the power again. We can only hope that he did not give any of them a heart attack. When the Squadron was reformed in 1946 Marcus was appointed in command with his old friend Dunlop Urie as a Flight Commander.

Shortly after he joined in 1934 Marcus was involved in an event which took place, and which must have been a nasty shock for the parents of the various officers in the Squadron. It had been decided to play a rugby match at Newcastle between the two Scottish Squadrons and 607 and 608 Squadrons. Five Harts set off for Usworth from Turnhouse and six from

Abbotsinch. Douglas Farquhar, with Sandy as passenger, was leading the 602 formation with Andrew Rintoul, Edward Howell, Hosier Hodge, John Shewell and Marcus. The clouds were down so they chose to hug the coast. Well down towards Berwick on Tweed they turned back in the face of a heavy snow storm to discover there was another snow storm coming in behind. It was every man for himself. Douglas landed on the beach at Joppa. He and Sandy tied their Hart to a lamp post with a length of rope provided by a neighbour; and then caught a tram into Edinburgh to make their report by telephone. Andrew Rintoul and Edward Howell scraped back into Turnhouse. Hosier Hodge landed but went on his nose. Shewell's Hart was a write off, leaving Marcus Robinson, still without his wings, to make the best of it. To his great credit he made a successful forced landing near Davidson's Mains, Edinburgh. 603 lost three of their Harts, but the Scottish team were lucky to have survived without injury. Douglas Farquhar, who took responsibility for the escapade, expected to be court martialled, but appears to have got away with it.

Sandy Johnstone in 'B' Flight and Dunlop Urie in 'A' Flight were about equally senior. John Hawkes and Alistair Grant were in 'C' Flight. As an architect practising in Inverness, Grant was at rather a disadvantage. One of us had to fly there to get him for his weekend camps. In due course David McIntyre offered Sandy a job as a pilot instructor in his school of navigation at Prestwick. The experience he thereby gained earned, both by day and by night, proved of great value to the Squadron.

In choosing E V N Bell, known as "Ding Dong", as his secretary, Clydesdale made a shrewd appointment. Ding Dong was soon recruited and commissioned in the Squadron. As a retired guards officer he provided a wealth of service experience which most of us lacked. Already in his thirties he proved a competent pilot, but when we changed to the Fighter roll he was gradually groomed to be our Auxiliary Adjutant in the event of war - a job for which he proved eminently suitable. He was soon moved on up to higher staff appointments.

The next three officers to be commissioned in 1936 were Findlay Boyd, Ian Ferguson and myself, followed later in the year by Archie McKellar and Donald Jack.

After leaving Sedbergh, Findlay was employed by his father to manage the family coal pit near Larkhall. Coalminers are not the easiest men to deal with, but he seems to have gained their co-operation and respect. He certainly picked up some of their colourful language which was much enjoyed by Norman Stone and myself. At Drem Findlay would invite us to go with him for a "donner" round the perimeter track. "I'll be in my scratcher" he used to say, meaning in his bed. I caught the habit and still enjoy lying in my scratcher.

Almost as bad as the Germans in Findlay's book were fox hunters, which was surprising because with a gun in his hand no grouse or pheasant in sight would be long for this world! I could scarcely believe a grouse enjoyed being killed any more than a fox which certainly had a better chance of escaping.

Findlay enforced strict discipline for others but made his own rules for himself. He was a powerful character and frequently difficult to live with, which was in contrast with the quiet well-mannered ways of Ian Ferguson, the best looking man in 'B' Flight. I never got to know Ian as well as I should. He was reserved in manner, keen on his flying, but an introvert by nature in strong contrast to Archie McKellar – the 'B' Flight extrovert.

Quite soon after McKellar became operational on Hinds we were all despatched to find and pinpoint different places in Scotland and to bring back evidence of our success by means of oblique photographs to be taken by our air gunners. Glamis Castle, the childhood home of Her Majesty the Queen, was allotted to Archie. He made a feast of it. When the photographic section produced the pictures for inspection by Reggie Dale, the Adjutant, to his embarrassment Archie's pictures revealed not only Glamis Castle, but close up through the bedroom windows complete with beds and furniture. All he seemed to have missed were the chamber pots!

Much has been written about Archie McKellar who was probably Scotland's greatest fighter pilot. I have added some further details and personal impressions about Findlay and Archie in the chapter devoted to the Battle of Britain.

D M Jack, sometimes referred to as "Donald Duck", was an old friend who was also inspired to join the Squadron by Edward Howell. His first problem was elderly parents who did not wish to see him airborne. His role would have to be limited to taxiing! I never heard how he got round that one. Donald and Archie made their appearance after the 1936 camp at Tangmere. I remember some rude speculation in the Mess as to whether Donald's long neck would stand up to the slip stream in the pilot's seat of the Hind without dislocation; but despite his friendly unwarlike appearance and character Donald probably did a longer stint of fighter operations than most of us. In 'A' Flight he went right through the first year of the war and the Battle of Britain, and then after a short rest on the staff at 13 Group, he raised and commanded 123 Squadron which he took to the Middle East. Later 123 amalgamated with 80 Squadron with Donald in command. He was to do a full eight months in the desert as a Squadron Commander. He survived to become in the words of one of his pilots:

"The finest fighter leader I ever served under and one of the greatest pilots never to win a medal. They should have given him the DSO. Later in the war some guys got it for less in the way of accumulated experience. Donald may not have had a single moment of glory but his courage and calmness throughout the campaign were an inspiration."

Donald's book "Flying Free" contains a wealth of detail about a wide range of RAF characters involved in our Middle East operations. At an early stage he and Edward Howell celebrated in Cairo Howell's escape after being made a prisoner leading the RAF rear guard operation after our defeat in Crete. This operation is described in "Escape to Live" by Wing Commander Edward Howell, OBE, DFC.

The early days would not be complete without reference to the unobtrusive and valuable efforts by our Padre and the Medical Officer, Squadron Leader Doc Allan.

The Reverend Louis Sutherland, Minister of the Holyrood Church in Stirling was, in spite

Hawker Hinds and 602 Squadron personnel at Tangmere in 1936

of his age, a regular attender at Abbotsinch where he kept us in touch with the airmen. This was a role some of us, including myself, tended to neglect. He was adept at sorting out human problems and, sometimes, investigating less creditable incidents for which we were not sufficiently experienced to deal with. Some of the Paisley residents did not appreciate the music of the Rolls Royce Kestrel engines on Sunday; so when the complaints began to mount Louis was sent to tell them that God was on our side!

Squadron Leader Doc Allan was associated with the Royal Alexandra Hospital in Paisley. He had served with the Royal Flying Corps in the Great War. Doc Allan was a taciturn, down-to-earth character with a fund of service experience. He was promoted to Wing Commander, and became Principal Medical Officer of 11 Group during the Battle of Britain. Doc Allan was the one to propose the Squadron motto - "Cave Leonem Cruciatum".

In the autumn of 1936 a number of junior officers were summoned to a levee at Holyrood House to make their bow to the Monarch in recognition of their commissions. Full dress uniforms were hired from Grieves in London and despatched to their Edinburgh branch who delivered them to the Gentlemen's Lavatory at Waverley Station. There we arrayed ourselves for the occasion. On arrival at Holyrood we assembled in the long gallery adorned by what must be a galaxy of phoney portraits of Scottish kings. We were closely guarded by the Royal Bodyguard with bows and arrows at the ready. It was for Archie the perfect setting for playing the fool and he took advantage of it. I had seated myself comfortably on the end of a heavy oak refectory table. Archie and his loathsome 'B' Flight accomplices perched themselves on the other end from which they suddenly nipped off. The table under my weight went down, see-sawing up at the other end which came down again with a frightful crash. Meanwhile I slid to the floor with an unholy clatter as my sword and helmet with its feather pom-pom hit the deck. The startled archers clutched their bows and fingered their clubs! Fortunately we were summoned before the scowling bodyguards could resort to their weapons. On our way through to the throne room we passed a small window overlooking the garden behind the Palace and were intrigued to see two wee girls running about on the grass - guess who! At the entrance to the throne room our cards were passed from hand to hand up a row of courtiers leading to His Majesty. This phalanx was supposed to coincide with the number of officers in the queue waiting to make their bow. It sounds easy but there was a panic. The queue was out of step with the cards. The Courtier beside the King was announcing the wrong names. Mark Selway who was in charge of the 602 contingent made a rapid assessment of the crisis and saved the situation by stepping out of the queue, thereby forfeiting his royal nod and saving ours! Quick thinking.

After making his bow to King George VI Archie had his photograph taken before returning his plumage to Gieves. The picture has been copied on his grave stone. He is thus recorded for posterity, "briefly clothed for his Royal encounter by courtesy of Gieves and the public conveniences in Waverley Station".

Paul Webb made his appearance at Abbotsinch on 25th April 1937. I was detailed to give him his first flight in the back of a Hind. We had some fun buzzing round a party of hill walkers on the top of Dumgoyne. The experience must have whetted his appetite for a commission in 602. He soon got the hang of it. He did, however, suffer a set back on his first cross country flight. Setting forth for Aberdeen in a Hind, about 40 minutes later Webb found himself over Newcastle! One may wonder how on earth he did it. The explanation was really quite simple. The bowl containing the pilot's compass was covered by a glass top with two parallel lines etched upon it. The glass top was fixed in a metal ring with its circumference marked out on the rim in the full circle of 360 degrees. The pilot would adjust the ring until the course he wanted to fly coincided with the fore and aft line of the aircraft. After that all one had to do was keep the compass needle between the parallel lines; but first it was

Royal Levée, Holyrood Palace, 1937
L-R: Marquess of Douglas & Clydesdale,
John Hawkes, David McIntyre, Sandy Johnstone,
Tony Muspratt-Williams

necessary to clamp down the ring which would otherwise begin to rotate with the vibration of the aeroplane. Paul forgot, or perhaps no one told him, to clamp the ring so instead of going to Aberdeen the ring gradually rotated causing him to fly in a huge semi circle finding himself unwilling and uninvited 'coal to Newcastle'. His first long cross country had not gone any better than mine to Speke.

Paul's performance in the Battle of Britain before he retired to St Richards Hospital at the end of August marked him out as a pilot who had the knack of using an aeroplane as a gun platform. He was later in the war awarded the DFC and a permanent commission in the RAF. He was made a CBE before retiring as an Air Commodore. I have included at Chapter 10 a brief account of our joint experience in hospital evacuation from St Richards to the Warnford Hospital in Leamington.

The next pilot to join was Nigel Graeme, an English son of an ancient Scottish family with military connections. He soon became a popular addition to 'B' Flight, but unfortunately his job in Glasgow came to an end so he returned to Newcastle where he rejoined 607 Squadron. Sadly he was killed early in the war.

I was on leave of absence overseas during the latter part of 1937 and early in 1938 when we recruited Norman "Twenty Stone", a large officer who combined a sharp legal mind and a ribald sense of humour. Like so many young Glasgow graduates he was initially bitten with socialism. With my public school background I feared we might become a case of oil and water. I need not have worried. As time went by he became bluer and bluer as I became pinker and pinker with disgust at the memory of Governments led by Stanley Baldwin and Neville Chamberlain, which had failed to rearm adequately in time to meet the obvious Hitler menace. In retrospect I may have been unfair. A realistic rearmament programme in the mid-thirties could have led to a political defeat. Far too many British people still had their heads buried firmly in the sand. If Labour had been returned in the pre war years I doubt if Britain would have survived. On the other side of the coin, if we had been properly prepared Hitler could well have hesitated and certainly would have hesitated if Winston Churchill had been at the helm. Young men such as Norman might have survived to play their part in the latter half of the Twentieth Century. Indeed, I had my eye on him as a possible partner in our firm when the war was over, but that was not to be.

When we met, Norman had already been in the newspapers. He had got himself lost in an Avro Tutor which he unsuccessfully landed near Kilsyth. For such a bright chap his bump of locality was poor. It must have been because he was full of praise for my sense of

41

direction. He was not one to waste time on massaging egos so I was quite chuffed, to use a modern expression. Orders from Group or Commands which did not make sense caused Norman to distrust arm chair warriors. His favourite butt was an imaginary Air Marshal giving orders from his swivel chair. "Throw in 602 and quick about it. Hold it, this damned chair is squeaking again. Send for works and bricks". Defusing pompous official administrators appealed to Norman. Marcus Robinson tells of a passage of arms in sick quarters while undergoing his routine medical examination by a languid and rather bored M.O. After blowing up the mercury and performing all the other contortions the Doc muttered "All right read the letters". After a pause Norman replied "What letters?" "The letters on the board, man". After another pause Norman looked round the room with a puzzled frown, and asked in a plaintive voice "What board?"

I never asked Norman whether he was agnostic or atheist in his beliefs, but I suppose it was the latter. He had a curious down on Spiritualists, and the late Sir Arthur Conon Doyle in particular. He was always going on about Conon. The splendid works of fiction by that outstanding author cut no ice with him, nor even the tenets of the New Testament. At Drem he painted on the fuselage of his aeroplane a ghostly white figure with the initials H.G. subscribed. In vain I told him no good would come of it. Soon after it was his tendency to put a Spitfire on its nose that resulted in his posting to Training Command to do an instructors course, which would make proper use of his education and articulate speech. I last saw Norman with his wife in November 1940 at a get together in the

Donald Jack, Findlay Boyd and Dunlop Urie relax at the 1939 summer camp at Church Fenton

Piccadilly Club, Sauchiehall Street, at which we learned with dismay that Archie McKellar had just been shot down and killed with 605 Squadron. Norman was later killed when his aircraft broke up during aerobatics. Fortunately he left a son who became a Professor of Modern History at Oxford University.

In 1939 we were joined by Sergeant Randall Phillips. Arthur Charret, the assistant adjutant, just managed to get him trained in time for mobilisation. He served a full tour of operations and was duly commissioned rising to the acting rank of Squadron Leader.

Hugh Glen Niven, the last very new boy, was not so lucky. On mobilisation he was posted to Training Command and did not return until the end of August 1940 in time to be thrown in at the deep end. Fortunately he survived the experience and was flying on ops long after the original pilots had gone elsewhere. In the end he collapsed in the mess after a fighter sweep over the Low Countries. The Docs pounced just in time and found him suffering from advanced TB. After several weary years in Tornadee, Aberdeenshire, he made a recovery. Glen has done more than any of us to keep all members of the Squadron, pre and post war, in touch. Without him as secretary it would have been very difficult to launch the 602 Museum project.

A few months before the war began we were joined by Pilot Officer R T (Rab) Richards, a purveyor of ready mix concrete with a surprising knowledge and understanding of machine guns. The Spitfire, with its shallow wings crammed full of wheels, oleo legs, eight Browning machine guns and ammunition belts, was a complicated firing platform lurking under the smooth streamlined exterior. How Mr Mitchell, the designer, found room for the main spars to stop the wings falling off still remains a mystery to me! Rab's appearance at Abbotsinch was an act of providence. Having mastered the complexities of our machine guns he studied the vital procedures for reloading and rearming them with minimum delay. Then lo and behold soon after the war began he designed and fitted a modification to the mechanism which almost halved the reloading and rearming time. This was soon adopted through Fighter Command. I can only hope he got some recognition for this vital service – but I doubt it!

The RAF must have recognised gold when they found it because Rab soon disappeared to fresh fields. We also lost touch with his wife, Mary, who had thrown herself into the breach during the period of mobilisation to decipher coded messages pending the appointment and training of WAAF officers for this unenviable task.

CHAPTER 4
1937/1939

On the retiral of Lord Clydesdale, after the camp at Tangmere in 1936, David McIntyre was the obvious man to succeed him as our Commanding Officer. In his brief career as an instructor he had demonstrated the usual degree of efficiency he brought to any task that came his way. It was typical that he got himself attached to a regular squadron in the RAF so as to brush himself up for the Everest Flight. His part in that enterprise is well worth reading in the Pilot's Book of Everest.

In his early days he did make some mistakes. George Pinkerton told me a tale of the 602 pilots sitting in the crew room at Renfrew in the early thirties with nothing to do but gaze out of the window at lashing rain driven by a near gale. To their disgust the sea gulls were still flying. Mac watched with interest their mode of landing on the tarmac. this was achieved by a steep dive about 45 degrees cross wind. At the last moment the gull would pull out of the dive and make a steep turn into wind rotating the angle of attack of its wings to the stalling point. At this stage the cross wind drift would be cancelled out by the gull's forward speed enabling it to step neatly on to the tarmac. Mac was fascinated. "If the gulls can do it so can I". Off he went in an Avro. He did the dive. He did the steep turn and pulled back the stick. He then landed but, sadly, not on his under carriage but upside down. Only an Auxiliary Pilot could have got away with that!

Getting out of jams and difficulties was where Mac excelled and gives an important clue to his later success in the business side of aviation. This ability was well illustrated by

Pilot Officer MacLean in Hawker Hind K5507 at Abbotsinch in May 1937

Marcus Robinson's story about McIntyre at the Lympne Camp in 1934. He borrowed the CO's private aeroplane for the weekend in order to visit his fiancée. Due to some unrecorded mishap the prop got broken. There was a young Scot in the far South of England with a broken private aeroplane far from suppliers of propellers for this type of aircraft. If found they would be closing down for the weekend. He was in the soup! Yet on Monday morning he was back for duty in Clydesdale's aeroplane complete with a new airscrew!

In July 1937 the Squadron flew into Rochford, a small aerodrome within walking distance of Southend-on-Sea. Just outside the eastern perimeter of the airfield was a railway, running north and south, with overhead wires exactly across the landing approach into the prevailing wind from the west. This rendered the aerodrome considerably shorter for landing which had to be done with as low an air speed as possible.

I am not sure who actually owned Rochford. There were no RAF buildings or personnel in evidence. It was, however, in use as a flying club complete with a club house and a drinking bar. These premises appeared to be occupied and manned by the chairman of the club who dispensed alcoholic refreshments. All seemed to be going well until suddenly we found ourselves *persona non grata* at the club. The story was that Mac had thought the chairman really was the barman. Unfortunately the chairman was not blessed with a sense of humour which might have saved the situation. So for the Squadron it was to your tents O Israel!

Once more Mac, proving himself as a man of infinite resource and sagacity made a messing deal with the Palace Hotel, Southend who did us proud at a very reasonable cost. The bar in the Palace Hotel sticks in my memory when we celebrated John Hawkes' escape from his first skirmish with the Reaper. He had come in rather low and not quite fast enough over that wretched railway. His wheels caught the wires and down he came inside the aerodrome on his nose. I think he lost a tooth. There followed a celebration in the Palace Hotel which involved the consumption of Pimms 1-2-3-4-3-2-1. I think I walked back to Rochford after watching Marlene Dietrich in the *Garden of Allah* showing at the local cinema, but I do not remember much about it.

In order to gain further experience in cross country flying and pin pointing targets I was despatched in an Avro Tutor, which cruised at about 85 miles per hour, to find and turn at several points in East Anglia. This sounded easy enough, but by the time I took off a 40 mile per hour cross wind had developed. The terrain in East Anglia proved dead flat with a complete absence of any discernible features. Despite the cross wind I found the points but could not be sure of Duxford as the last one on my itinerary. A likely airfield came into view so I landed and taxied up to the watch office. A keen young airman dashed out and I asked him to bring me a glass of water. After a brief friendly conversation and a few leading questions I was satisfied that I had indeed arrived at Duxford which enabled me to report mission accomplished, albeit it in a somewhat devious manner!

Rochford was a good experience for the Squadron because we were all under canvas which was good training for war time conditions.

After Rochford we were invited to Mac's house in the country near Prestwick to celebrate

The annual camp at Rochford in 1937 was the first occasion on which the Squadron officers wore their new mess kit. Permission to wear the Grey Douglas kilt had just been granted. Gathered here at the Palace Hotel, Southend-on-Sea are:
Standing – Muspratt-Williams; ?; Urie; Dale; Boyd; MacLean; Allan; Robinson; McKellar; Jack; Tindal; Sutherland; Hawkes; Ferguson; Johnstone
Seated – Grant; Bell; McIntyre; Farquhar; Feather; Pinkerton

46

the christening of his son. The party developed with the usual Squadron gusto. Then the time came to light a huge but reluctant bonfire in the shape of a haystack waiting for us in the garden. Dusk fell but no flames arose so I rolled up and lit a paper brand and advanced upon the target. Suddenly there were cries of alarm. Human figures cascaded down from the bonfire which to my amazement burst into flames. The mystery was resolved about 2.00 a.m. in the following morning when Donald Jack and I ran out of petrol which had been siphoned out of the petrol tank in my car. We would have made Abbotsinch but missed the way and found ourselves in Ochiltree. It seemed a nice enough looking place but not looking at its best at 2.00 a.m. I have never been back to Ochiltree by daylight. Following our retreat from Ochiltree we ran out of petrol and were rescued on the Gleniffer Braes by Donald's brother Tom armed with a can of

petrol. For me and those on the bonfire it had been a near squeak. Mac had a keen sense of humour, but he would have drawn the line at having his guests cremated whether guilty or not guilty of misappropriation my petrol.

By September 1937 Mac had become more and more involved with flying training at Prestwick. The command of the Squadron passed to Andrew Douglas Farquhar.

By this time I had completed my legal training and took advantage of a sabbatical leave of absence from the profession to go round the world, with leave from the Squadron, and by agreement with my father who had reluctantly agreed to pay the price of the frolic. It took eight months and cost just over £300. It was a wonderful experience which I knew could never be repeated once I became truly involved in legal practice.

Squadron Leader A D Farquhar
Commanding Officer Oct 1937 – Apr 1940

When I became air borne again on 6th June 1938 I had only done 126 hours solo with 32 hours dual and passenger flights. More effort would be needed to catch up before our next camp. This took place at RAF Station Hawkinge which occupied a small aerodrome in the south downs quite near Eastbourne. As we approached to land I noted an odd looking white hole in the chalk escarpment to the south of the airfield. I was later told that this was where Connel Law, a Kilmacolm friend, had ended his short career in the Royal Air Force.

Those who flew with me as air gunners at Hawkinge were Slorance, Wood, Conway, Outch, Hempkin, Collins, Third, Anderson and Perfect. The last mentioned enjoyed the double bonus of a forced landing at Wilmington, a new aerodrome under construction somewhere near Brighton. Before breakfast we had taken off into the lovely smooth morning air; but as the flight progressed up rose the fog covering all the downs. I hurried back towards Hawkinge but the haar was already down on the sea. Turning tail I raced westwards for refuge while there was still some ground to see, and then saw Wilmington. Pronto down I went. Once on terra firma I left Perfect to guard the Hind and presented myself at a nearby house in order to phone Douglas Farquhar at Hawkinge. The lady in the house insisted I should stay for breakfast, so ungallantly I left my air gunner to his guard duties. Later in the day the fog lifted; but if I had not gone down at Wilmington I might well have been in trouble.

LAC Perfect himself was no stranger to forced landings. On this occasion, he did at least do it in the aeroplane and not by parachute as he did on his famous descent near Loch Lomond from the bomb aimers compartment of a Hawker Hart, which George Pinkerton was flying in an army co-operation exercise. At the subsequent inquiry Perfect claimed that he had got his feet tangled up with the elevator control wires which ran through the bomb aimers cockpit, and then mistook George's frantic signals to get clear of his flying controls as an order to bale out! I next met Perfect during the war in a London tube station attired, rather to my surprise, as a Wing Commander. He told me he had been in command of a Bomber Squadron; *C'etait la Guerre!*

Wilmington gave me quite a turn. It made me wonder when we would get RT (radio telephone) in our aeroplanes. Soon after that we did; but the equipment was a hopeless flop - just a few gargling voices hushed by scratching atmospherics. We breathed a sigh of relief when the sets just disappeared.

The Hawkinge camp was much occupied by flights to the ranges at Eastchurch where the air gunners also got a chance to blast off. Like the pilots they suffered from stoppages.

The pilots' guns were synchronised with the propeller which would get in the way and get shot off if the engine was allowed to drop below 1600 revs. More difficult were the four different causes of a stoppage. As a newly promoted Flying Officer I was supposed to have mastered the art of clearing them. Stoppage number four required a hammer, a tool not normally carried by a pilot. The remedy was supposed to be found by removing a shoe and hammering the offending part with the heel. I did not try it! This carry on made me wonder how the RFC, with propeller synchronised machine guns, ever managed to shoot anything down in the Great War. All the more credit to them that they did such a magnificent job.

My last memory of 1938 was my first solo by night over the Empire Exhibition at Bellahouston Park. Suddenly I was illuminated by a blinding searchlight which flooded the cockpit, obliterating my view of the instruments. I hope those on the ground enjoyed the experience more than I did! The Exhibition was fun and the Palace of Engineering a great success. When it closed, David McIntryre, the great opportunist, took the Palace of Engineering lock, stock and barrel down to Prestwick where it became his star hanger and work shop.

By the end of 1938 Andrew Douglas Farquhar (Douglas as he was called) had been in command for just over a year which was to be the end of 602 as a Light Bomber Squadron. Douglas, a Glasgow stockbroker by profession, was a confident, intelligent man in his early thirties when he was appointed to command. In retrospect he was so quick in the uptake that he tended to make impulsive decisions. He could also be rather scathing towards those not quite so proficient as himself. "I never have any trouble" was his frequent reaction. His verbal repartee was fast and delivered with a keen sense of humour. After flying on Saturday evening he gave some of us a lift to Glasgow for our traditional binge in Roganos. Driving into Hendersons Garage in West Nile Street we were halted at the entrance by a lugibuous figure in a brown overall. Douglas leaned out of the window and declared in stentorian tones. "I know, don't tell me. There isn't any room. There never was any room and there never will be any room". The attendant was so shaken that he let us in.

On assuming command in September 1937 Douglas began a campaign with Number 6 Auxiliary Group and the Air Ministry. In the end he succeeded in convincing the RAF that a bombing role for 602 was inappropriate. To train a bomber crew the aeroplane had to have a realistic operational range. The Hind was a lovely little aircraft but had to be refuelled even to reach the south coast of England with a safety margin of fuel in its tanks. Large aircraft and longer flights were not so suitable for those who had civilian jobs to do. The

Hind with a cruising speed of 140 miles an hour was clearly out of date except for dive bombing. Moreover new aircraft such as the Wellington, the Hampden and the Stirling were reaching the point of delivery. It was, therefore, not surprising that by November 1938 Douglas was seen to have made his point; but the authorities got the better of him. To our amazement and disappointment we were to be an Army Co-operation Squadron. The Hinds were withdrawn and to everyone's surprise we were re-equipped with the Hawker Hector which was really just a Hind and an 800 horse power Napier engine with 24 cylinders arranged in the form of an 'H'. John Hawkes was the only man with a good word for the Hector. After his first flight he described the aircraft's ability to climb as "like a fart in a bath"!

It is difficult to conceive a more unsuitable role for an Auxiliary Squadron on the verge of war. We had no knowledge of army tactics and how we might fit in. To my knowledge no soldier was ever seen at Abbotsinch except John Millman, a pal of mine, who was a regular adjutant in the H.L.I. He was sick all over the back of the Hind including my spare dungarees. After that I gave up Army Co-operation!

The first official step for all Army Co-op pilots was to learn Morse code for communicating with the ground by W.T. This order proved unpopular. Very little effort was made to obey, nor did Douglas make much effort to enforce a task which was too much to ask from officers with full time civilian jobs as well as flying. In due course Wing Commander Porter of 60 Group, an elderly Signals Officer, was sent to examine the boys on their Morse code. It was an awkward confrontation - polite smiles but no Morse code!

Douglas was quick off the mark. Down he went to London, and shoe horned himself into the presence of Air Marshal Sholto Douglas to whom he explained the facts of life! Whether it was due to this confrontation, or Porter's report I do not know; but the decision which followed was that 602 should be a single seater Fighter Squadron. It was the right decision for us, and the right decision for Fighter Command. The only losers were our air gunners, and members of the Squadron who had enjoyed a trip in the back of the light bombers.

About this time the RAF decided that it would help us in darkened cockpits for the hills and mountains on service maps to be hatched purple instead of the traditional brown shades. All maps were to be handed in. The order was immediately obeyed, but to our surprise no new maps were handed out, and nothing happened for at least six weeks during which we were mapless. It was rude awakening to the British capacity for official bungling which became evident in many such incidents in the future, including the incredible story rumoured of the 200 Blenheim air screws requested during the war by Headquarters Middle East who were much embarrassed when 200 Blenheim air crews arrived after their long and dangerous journey round the Cape of Good Hope. One hopes it was just a rumour.

In February 1939 our brief encounter with the Hawker Hector came to an end with the arrival of the Gloster Gauntlet, a sprightly little bi-plane which looked as though it had been left over from the Somme. It had a most complicated petrol ignition system whereby the pilot manufactured his mixture and twiddled a wee knob to ignite it. If it did not work you did not fly, but when you did the Gauntlet was exceptionally manoeuvrable and a joy in the air. It could do over 200 miles an hour and was complete with a rather inefficient RT, and oxygen. I see from my log book that I reached 30,000 feet for the first time.

On April 30th A Flight gave a formation display culminating with a Prince of Wales Feathers over Hamden Park where the crowds were waiting for an important match to start. May 7th was not so good. My engine cut shortly after a formation take off right above high grid pylons over the River Cart. I was lucky to land back on the aerodrome with a dead prop. - No 2 life gone!

Empire Air day took place on May 20th. The Gauntlets were just the ticket for showing off, but nothing could compare with the nail biting display of low level aerobatics given by Nick Tindal, our Assistant Adjutant, in a Hawker Demon.

After a few drinks in the mess we set off for a dance at Ballykinrain Hotel near Balfron accompanied by our chosen partners. Dunlop Urie and our guest Colin Fleming both aimed to be first to arrive in their fast motor cars. Surging up from Erskine Ferry, on the north bank of the Clyde, Dunlop was leading the field, shooting across the hump backed opening bridge over the Forth and Clyde Canal. Colin from behind observed a large object detach itself from the Urie motor car which spun away through the air. Dunlop ground to a halt, perhaps the only motorist who lost his petrol tank crossing a canal.

Later on at the end of the party I myself became the next casualty. Just as the last of the guests were driving off the family car which I had borrowed for the occasion, completely failed to start. The hotel was closing and had no accommodation, so there I was in mid Stirlingshire at one o'clock a.m. with Ruby Metcalf, my partner, waiting to be delivered safely back to her parents in Glasgow. I tinkered with the engine without success; but to my amazement help just appeared out of the blue. A large car driven by Percy Walker, a young medical student who had been at the party with two friends, suddenly drew up. "We are going to climb Ben Nevis" he said, "but I have left my alarm clock behind." I was prepared to clutch at any straw and explained our predicament. "Not to worry" said Walker, "when I've got that clock I'll drive Ruby back to Glasgow and you back to Abbotsinch", and so he did before they set off for Ben Nevis. St Christopher himself could not have done more. They don't come higher than Doctor Percy Walker with or without an alarm clock!

After this frolic our Gauntlets were gradually replaced by Spitfires. These began to arrive in April and May 1939. Douglas became a proud man in command of the first Auxiliary Squadron to get them. I think I am correct in making this claim, but I am equally certain it was the size of Abbotsinch which was the crucial deciding factor. Regular squadrons based on aerodromes with shorter landing and take off space must have envied the Scottish Amateurs with their huge landing ground.

By this time, of course, the RAF expansion was under way. All kinds of keen new boys were coming in, not only from Britain but from the Dominions. Except for the hard core of senior RAF regulars this expansion had the effect of making us more or less comparable in experience with the regular squadrons.

As things turned out the RAF got it right. The Spitfire needed space. Although beautiful in the air it could be a cow on the muddy ground. Before touch down the long nose had to rise which blotted out the view ahead. The centre of gravity was probably too far forward which made it liable to tip forward on its nose with damage to the prop.

Most of us were flying Spitfires in time for our last camp at Church Fenton on 15th July 1939.

In the meantime Alastair Grant and I had been on holiday in Norway from 24th June to 11th July visiting my relations there, and motoring around the Fjords in my Austin 8. It was to be the last chance of a holiday abroad for the next six years.

Every time we came down from the mountains to another lovely Fjord there would be the same large German liner lying at anchor. The passengers never came ashore. When we enquired about this vessel our naive Norwegian hosts would tell us with admiration in their voices that it was a German strength through joy cruise! The strength was yet to come, but not much joy. The cruise was obviously just a means of planning a future campaign.

Church Fenton which had been chosen in the Great War by my uncle Campbell as an aerodrome for the RFC was a busy RAF sector station in Fighter Command. It was occupied by a Blenheim Squadron and No 72, a crack regular Fighter Squadron, still equipped with Gladiators. Here we had our first real experience of flying under the new system of sector control devised by "Stuffy" Dowding, the Commander in Chief. The HF (High Frequency)

RT worked tolerably well during daylight. Valuable experience was gained.

I suspect most of the Blenheim boys were just blown to bits quite early in the war in those idiotic daylight raids over Kiel, and other sensitive German bases. We were to see more of 72 in due course at Drem. Annual training culminated with a guest night at which we were given permission to wear our new mess kit, complete with the Grey Douglas kilt worn by courtesy of our former Commanding Officer, now His Grace the Duke of Hamilton and Brandon. This Grey Douglas was his private tartan and went well with the blue mess kit uniform jackets. Needless to say those low minded regulars wanted to know what went on underneath, which resulted in a fairly rough conclusion to the evening!

The flight back to Abbotsinch on the 29th July was to be the last time the Squadron took the air before mobilisation into the RAF.

CHAPTER 5
REGULARS

No account of 602 would be complete without paying due tribute to the Regular Officers, NCOs and airmen of the RAF who did our administration, and supervised the maintenance and training of the airmen. They served us well. Above all they taught us to fly, and even managed to turn us into officers for the Royal Air Force.

The senior pilots of the Squadron had either been taught to fly at the Scottish Flying Club, or by the Regular Adjutant, Flight Lieutenant Hodson an RFC pilot who is remembered as a calm, able instructor. Hoddy who rose to the rank of Air Vice Marshall in the war was succeeded, a few years before I joined, by Anthony (known as Mark) Dunmore Selway, a Cranwell graduate with considerable ability and with plenty of initiative which he never hesitated to use. He could be exasperated by the bumbling and bull of the service but managed to stay reasonably relaxed in spite of the additional work imposed upon him as Adjutant to an absent Station Commander. Mark never failed to see the humorous side of any situation. His efforts to make Abbotsinch acceptable for night flying led to a hilarious conclusion. The difficulty lay with Bow McLachlan, a company which operated a foundry just across the road from the guardroom gate, with a chimney stalk about 250 feet high. After many months of negotiation with the Air Ministry a red light was fixed to the top of this dangerous obstruction. Soon after Bow McLachlan closed down and demolished the factory. When Mark asked them why the chimneystack was still standing they replied in rather an injured tone "But surely you need that for your light"!

With the aerodrome now acceptable for night flying the Air Ministry decided to develop Abbotsinch as a regular RAF station. Bessonau hangers sprouted up. These were large fabric erections, hoop shaped with sloping sides and square ends fitted with opening doors for the aircraft. The first of these ended in disaster. It had been stupidly sited with the square opening end facing west into the prevailing wind instead of the sloping side. Abbotsinch is sited at the junction of two valleys, one running down to Ayrshire followed by the railway, and the other down the course of the River Clyde. These two valleys can produce a funnelling effect which can accelerate the force of a south-westerly gale. Of course, this had to happen with the result that the first hanger just flew off like a box kite. It landed on top of the Seageants" Mess which survived the impact without harm. When Mark made his inspection the hanger and its contents, including some Hinds of No 33 Squadron, were gone. The only remaining Air Ministry property he could report were two neat rows of red fire extinguishers!

Notwithstanding this set back a riot of single storey buildings soon sprang up to create a sizeable RAF base for a Coastal Command Reconnaissance Squadron in addition to 602 and any other unit they cared to send.

Wing Commander Brian Baker, DSO MC DFC, an RFC ace with 39 victories in the Great War was appointed Station Commander. He turned out to be an auxiliary enthusiast which made matters much easier than they might have been. Baker kept himself fit and used to play squash with me by courtesy of the late D S Carson in his court at Kilmacolm. Despite my obvious advantage in age I only just managed to beat him! In due course Brian Baker was promoted and took command of the important war station at Leuchars. He was succeeded by another RFC pilot, Group Captain Jones.

With a career at stake one could scarcely blame a regular officer for playing safe. Not so Mark who firmly believed in giving the Auxiliaries every opportunity for developing their experience and competence. Fortunately he did not get landed with Douglas Farquhar's rugby match, but despite that debacle he was ready to co-operate when Marcus Robinson requested permission to fly over to Arran where his parents were on holiday. There was a problem because the island had no landing field. "See if you can find one," said Mark, "and if you are quite sure land and picket the aircraft so that it does not blow away". Marcus duly found a field and made a safe landing. The farmer was not too happy but the matter was settled for a landing fee of five shillings. "You might have killed a sheep" was the farmer's surly comment.

If things had gone wrong it would have been a serious situation for Mark who had little to gain and much to lose.

Mark Selway served as a Squadron Commander in the Middle East during the war winning the D.F.C. Afterwards he rose rapidly in the RAF to become Commander in Chief in the Far East in the rank of Air Marshall.

In October 1936 Mark Selway was succeeded as Regular Adjutant by Flight Lieutenant Hilary Reginald (Regie) Dale. The RAF could not have found a better man for the job. Not only was he near perfection as a pilot, and as an instructor, but he also mastered the art of leadership which was almost unnoticed in the firm and friendly manner in which it was exercised. Moreover he was an auxiliary enthusiast. Regie was an immediate success. We took to him and he took to us. He was soon joined as Assistant Adjutant by Flight Lieutenant Nicolas Tindal, a colourful aerobatics pilot who could hold the crowds spell bound with his breath taking aerobatics. It was a joy to fly with Regie, but you had to get used to Nick's eccentricities. One of his passengers got out of the dual Hart looking a bit shaken. "Nick", he asked, "why did we have to come all the way back from Prestwick upside down"? "It's my piles old boy" he replied. "Inverted flying supposed to be good for them, drains out the blood you see"!

Nick should have been a Fighter Pilot but he was later posted to Bomber Command and finished the war in a prison camp. In my opinion he would have been a real asset in Fighter Command.

I will always be grateful to Regie for getting me out of a real mess. My aunt Hope in Strathblane invited me to a tennis party one Saturday afternoon. I had to refuse the invitation because of flying, but on my way back from a flight I decided to give them a buzz. Alighting from my Hind at Abbotsinch there was a message for me to see the Adjutant at once. Regie seemed to know the time and place and the culprit. "You know the rules about low flying." "Yes, I do." I told him about the party. "Well what makes it worse is a complaint by a neighbour. It appears that his housekeeper was having a baby." "Seems odd" I remarked. "That's none of your business," said Regie "the trouble is you accelerated the birth." Well there I was, as Norman Stone would have put it, "Doon the stank and round the bend beyond even the reach of Harpic". "I'll try and fix it" said Regie, and he did.

In due course I thanked him for his efforts. "You are lucky" he said, "I got into a similar mess myself out in Khartoum. The army were having a five star general inspection complete with colours, brass bands and cavalry. Like yourself I decided that an RAF contribution would brighten up the proceedings. Unfortunately the cavalry bolted, the troops and the band got into a tangle and the chaos reigned. The General was not amused. The Court Martial sentenced me with six months lost seniority."

After I was wounded Regie was given command of a Night Bomber Squadron and asked me to be his adjutant. It was a tempting offer which I felt bound to refuse because I thought my experience in fighters would be more usefully employed in Fighter Command. Soon after Regie Dale was shot down and killed over Germany. As a member of his team it would have been hard for me to bear.

After Regie's spell with 602 Flight Lieutenant Horace Stanley Darley was appointed adjutant on 6th July 1938 together with Plt Off Arthur Charret as his assistant. Findlay Boyd kept referring to our new adjutant as "Darnley", but almost before the matter was cleared up to his satisfaction Darley had been posted as adjutant of a Squadron at Speke. Thereafter he distinguished himself in command of 609 Squadron at Warmwell during the Battle of Britain and was awarded the DSO. He retired as a Group Captain in 1959.

Flight Lieutenant Cyril Hodder became our regular adjutant in December 1938. He must have had an anxious time during which the Squadron's role changed twice; first to Army Co-operation and then to Fighters. Soon after our brief conversion to Gauntlets the Spitfires began to arrive, fortunately accompanied by Joe Lewis (I think that was his name) a Test Pilot from Supermarine the manufacturers. Lewis had his hands full. Few of us had flown a monoplane, far less one with flaps or with a retractable undercarriage and a choice between fine or coarse pitch propellers. The Air Ministry supplied us with a dual control Fairey Battle for instruction in these mysteries. The task confronting Lewis and Hodder was further complicated when Dunlop Urie tangled with the flashing beacon while landing the Battle which was rendered unserviceable and beyond early repair for want of a spare part. War was imminent so the best the RAF could do for Hodder was to send him a Miles Magister so that we could learn about flaps. This was scarcely the answer. Lewis then prescribed a three hour written examination on the ways and means of flying a Spitfire. So back we went to our homework on the Supermarine manuals. I think we all duly passed the written examination, but soon began to realise that there was a marked difference between theory and practice.

As time went by there were stupid incidents, such as going on your nose, and more seriously forgetting to lower the undercarriage, which you could not see, before landing. Indeed Supermarine anticipated that one by providing a warning light and a horn which blew if the landing flaps were down and the wheels still up. The story is told of a pilot in another squadron sitting upside down in the cockpit of his crashed Spitfire with a puzzled frown on his face, enquiring how on earth it had happened. The horn was still blowing but he had never heard it before so had taken no notice. Failure to heed or trust warning indicators and devices has always been, and probably always will be, an endemic weakness among pilots.

Going on your nose was the most common accident with the Spitfire. The thousand horse power Rolls-Royce Merlin engine was really mounted too far forward of the wheels which made the aeroplane nose heavy on the ground. This normally did not matter if the pilot was careful with his brakes, but could be lethal for the aeroplane if you ran into mud or a soft patch. Then even a careless touch on the brakes could send you right over on your nose.

Another problem with the Spitfire was the undercarriage which was manually raised and lowered by a hefty black lever on the starboard side of the cockpit brought into action by a small metal selector switch situated below the throttle quadrant, which could not be seen without looking down. To activate the pump the pilot had to take his right hand off the control column and replace it with his left hand while pumping. Without a hand on the throttle it would return to the closed position with an alarming loss of power just after take off if the pilot had omitted to tighten the control on the throttle quadrant. Needless to say it was unlikely to happen more than once; but once was enough! Hand pumping procedure was ill suited for taking off on instruments by night. Even by day until one got used to finding the metal switch its sharp edge could result in a scratch and bleeding on the back of the left hand while fumbling for it. This was known as "Spitfire hand"; easily avoided after the initial experience. Seeing blood at tea time in the mess the CO enquired how we had come by these wounds. "Spitfire hand" I replied explaining the cause. "I never have any trouble" was Douglas Farquhar's typical reply.

Despite my success in the three hour examination I made a mess of my first take off, getting into a muddle between fine and course pitch. Fortunately with the aid of a thousand horse power from Rolls-Royce and plenty of space at Abbotsinch I survived this folly rising in triumph over the high grid pylons across the confluence of the Gryffe and the Black Cart rivers, pumping feverishly. Almost at once I was streaking across Bearsden at what seemed a phenomenal speed. After that it was pure joy. I even remembered to lower my undercarriage and the landing flaps. Cyril Hodder was not impressed. He would have to consider whether I was fit for further flying in a Spitfire. Fortunately it all came right two days later.

On mobilisation Ding Dong took over as Adjutant from Hodder who was posted to Bomber Command. Sad to say he was, in due course, shot down and killed in action.

In 1935 Flight Sergeant Staples was the regular maintenance high priest in the hangers. Fortunately he was on hand when an Avro with its engine ticking over suddenly burst into flames. Seizing a fire extinguisher Staples dashed out, tripped and fell. As he went down the button got pressed leaving poor Staples writhing in foam on the ground. Apart from the burning Avro it was not without its humorous aspect. Flight Sergeant Staples was succeeded by Flight Sergeant Tom Kent, a highly efficient engineer who entertained doubts about the value of the Auxiliary Air Force with its officers using his aeroplanes like a glorified flying club. Fortunately he stayed with us when the war was declared and remained for many months as the backbone of our aircraft maintenance. He must also have played his part in bringing on our own invaluable Senior Auxiliary NCOs, such as Flight Sergeant Thomson and Sergeant Henderson. Later I was able to justify our existence for Tom Kent when I taxied up to his hanger at Drem with a bullet hole through the perspex canopy over the cockpit. He cursed the Germans; but it did in its way bring the war into the hanger.

The last time I met Tom Kent was at Sydenham Aerodrome, Belfast, where he was in charge of the Headquarters Communications Flight. As a Staff Officer of the Northern Ireland Command (RAFNI) I did most of my visiting by air; but without any experience on twin engine aircraft my flying was restricted to the lowly Tiger Moth instead of the Oxfords flown by the other members of Air Staff. Without training the best I could do was to thumb a ride with Wing Commander Jack Riddle to see how he did it. In due course I presented myself at Sydenham and boarded one of our Oxfords in a state of funk with my knees shaking. I opened up the throttles to take off. Almost at once the Oxford swerved violently towards the control tower. I pulled off a pint on the port throttle and round she went the other way, and so on after a series of half pints into the Irish air. I prayed that no one had seen, but on looking round over my shoulder I saw Tom Kent sitting in the back.

He had no reason to be there and offered no explanation. I suspect he may have become aware of the quaking husk inside the Squadron Leader's uniform at Sydenham, and out of loyalty just nipped into the back of the Oxford to share my fate. I hardly liked to thank him. He was master of invective which could have been rather embarrassing. I had thus became double breasted which is as they used to call twin engine pilots.

With the Spitfires came Warrant Officer McIntosh to keep an overall eye on their maintenance. He soon disappeared during the early months of the war at Drem, and was thereafter seen as a Wing Commander; not quite like Venus from the foam but just about as rapid!

CHAPTER 6
MOBILISATION/WAR DECLARED

In August 1939 the Squadron was stood down as usual during that month after the summer camp. Our mess at Abbotsburn was closed so while my parents were away on holiday I decided to say in the regular mess at Abbotsinch which had now become the principal RAF base in the West of Scotland, and the rallying point for mobilisation of the Reserves in the event of war.

I came back from the office in Glasgow on the 14th August and was greeted at the door of the Mess by Arthur Charret, "How does it feel like to be in the RAF?" he asked. I replied as politely as I could that I did not feel like it at all because I was an Auxiliary. "Not since 3.00 this afternoon" he said. And so it was, but we never took off the 'A's off our uniforms. I went to bed that night with a sense of relief and exhilaration. Here was something definite at last.

Quite quickly during the next few days our airmen reported for duty, and the officers' mess at Abbotsburn was reopened for the last time. Camp kit, blankets and gas masks were issued together with a .38 revolver. None of them were ever used by me. Provisional arrangements were made to move the Spitfires to a dispersal site at the north-east side of the aerodrome with the operational teams under canvas just across the fence from a small farmhouse between the aerodrome and the road.

During that period the busiest man in the Squadron was a Flight Lieutenant (Cappy) Marshall, an ex regular army officer posted to us earlier in the year as Equipment Officer to succeed Major Palmer who had been added to our strength in 1938. Marshall and Doc Allan disappeared in due course after we settled in at Drem.

The regulars departed almost at once leaving Douglas and Ding Dong in full control. The Squadron was put on a readiness state in case of surprise attack.

At this time my brother Bruce McLean, aged 19, was staying with a German family in Frankfurt learning the language. My mother wrote telling him to come home at once but received a reply telling her not to worry. Surely those on the spot knew best! I dashed up to the GPO at Paisley and despatched a telegram "in uniform come at once". He left Reich with an hour to spare before all British nationals were forbidden to leave.

Soon after mobilisation 269, the Coastal Command Squadron, disappeared with their Ansons to a better tactical base. Abbotsinch became the hub of activity as the principal mustering point for the Reservists who started to stream through the gates. 602 found themselves doing all kinds of station duties including the decoding of signals, an art of which we knew little or nothing. I had one evening at Town Headquarters doing codes two years previously, so was despatched to the guard room to combine this task with the reception of the reservists. Towards evening Douglas and Ding Dong came to read the signals, but all I could show them was a large pile of paper and two or three rather badly decoded messages containing piffling details such as a lost Tiger Moth down in England. Some ass at Air Ministry had failed to cancel coding except for secret messages. This was a real worry because in that pile were vital instructions, such as the new war time call signs. I was glad to hand over the code books to the next man. This problem was neatly handled by Douglas who enlisted the aid of certain officers wives who soon cleared the backlog. This work was in due course undertaken by a special branch of the Women's Auxiliary Air Force.

Tony Musprat-Williams duly reported to take part in the anticipated hostilities, but no sooner had he set foot in Abbotsburn than a signal came from Air Ministry with lightning speed stopping his pay on account of an unpaid mess bill. With all the turmoil of mobilisation in progress it was almost beyond belief. What chance would Hitler have against such an Organisation!

Sprat ran true to form. He arrived to see off Hitler accompanied by Mickey Mouse and Villa, a bull terrier bitch. He was also accompanied by two rough looking young male friends at a loose end waiting their cue to join the war when it came. They were at once named Sprat's gorillas. As there was nothing in King's Regulations to forbid their presence Douglas Farquhar, who had other matters on his mind, took little notice. In due course the gorillas left Abbotsinch to deal with the enemy in their respective rolls.

At this juncture four new trained pilots arrived from the RAF Volunteer Reserve (RAFVR) at Prestwick. Pilot Officer Glyn Ritchie, Sergeant McDowall, Sergeant Bryden and Sergeant Macadam. They were reputed operational on Spitfires, and we were glad to see them.

Almost at once the dead hand of petrol rationing clamped down on the British people. The allocation for my Austin 8 was to be five gallons per month making me a virtual prisoner at Abbotsinch for the duration. We all applied for extra petrol, but were all refused except Ding Dong. He was good enough to show us how the application forms should be completed. His experience in the Guards had shown him just how the official minds worked in such cases with the result that we got enough extra to cope.

601 (County of London) Squadron at Hendon solved their petrol problems in an unique manner. Their CO Loel Guiness, who was well endowed with this world's goods, had a bright idea. He stopped at a small garage near Hendon aerodrome gate and had a word with the proprietor who was full of gloom about his prospects under petrol rationing. Without further ado Guiness made him an offer for the garage, lock stock and barrel, complete with 800 gallons of petrol in the tanks. The man was delighted and so were 601!

Meanwhile the situation in Europe got worse. The only happy events at Abbotsinch were provided by Dunlop Urie, Findlay Boyd and Donald Jack who married their fiancees. Dunlop and Donald set up their married homes in caravans parked quite near the aerodrome.

Then came the astounding news. Hitler had patched up a secret treaty with Russia, the very country he had promised to destroy in his book. Nothing could save Poland now, and nothing did.

The Russians would in due course learn, as Shakespeare put it, "that he who sups with the devil has need of a long spoon". In the end Hitler and his thugs would be sorry they had not paid attention to the words of Bismarck. When asked what he considered to be the greatest strategic factor on the world's stage, Bismarck is said to have answered "The fact that North America speaks English". He was proved right, not just once but twice.

WAR DECLARED
As Recalled by Marcus Robinson and Hector MacLean

It was Sunday morning 3rd September 1939 in the ante-room of the Auxiliary Officers mess Abbotsburn House, Abbotsinch. A small group of 602 Squadron officers were tensely awaiting the Prime Minister's statement. He was due to speak at 11.15 am Millions of people in Britain with radios must have been tuned in. With incredible incongruity the BBC was treating us to a talk on how to manage our cigarette card collections! "Don't bend your cards" - "Don't thumb your cards" pleaded the speaker in a frustrated broken voice. Then the BBC pulled themselves together and phased him out. Such was the banal and almost absurd overture prescribed by British Broadcasting for this crucial moment in the history of the Twentieth Century!

After a pregnant pause the Prime Minster, Neville Chamberlain began. He spoke briefly of the Ultimation the Government had sent to Hitler demanding an undertaking that Germany would withdraw her troops from Poland and cease their fighting there.

"I have to tell you" he said "No such undertaking has been received and consequently a state of war now exists between this country and Germany".

These fatal words were followed by the National Anthem. We arose and stood to attention rather sheepishly, and perhaps with some embarrassment.

Fg Off A Grant & Fg Off H MacLean beside one of 602's Spitfire Mk.Is at Abbotsinch in September 1939

The BBC struck up some stirring martial music. One hardly knew what to say, if anything. Someone commented rather facetiously "Well things must be bad" - then the silence was broken by Norman Stone. "Never change a winning team" was his hopeful quip - No doubt with our defeat of Germany in 1918 in his mind.

Archie McKellar relieved the tension in a mock plaintive voice. "I only joined for the dancing". On further reflection he turned to Norman, "What do you think we'll be going in 20 years time?" Norman's reply went something like this.

"We will be down at the Cenotaph. Some unctuous prelate will be sounding off about the sacrifices made by those who fought for freedom. Then we'll shuffle off back to the Lodging House wishing we had an arse to our trousers".

The mirth was soon quenched by a cold douche from George Pinkerton (who had been dubbed "Grumpy" after one of the dwarfs in Snow White because of his dour nature) - "Well boys" he said, "your life expectancy has just been reduced by about 30 years"!

Then the sirens wailed in London; but it wasn't the Luftwaffe; just the first of many false alarms.

CHAPTER 7
ABBOTSINCH/DREM

It was hard to conceive a more unsuitable base than Abbotsinch for the fighter defence of the West of Scotland with its engineering and shipbuilding industries so vital to the war effort. It was not only in the wrong place from a tactical point of view, but was situated in the centre of an anti aircraft gun area surrounded by balloons, fitted with explosive devices in their cables.

The Air Ministry effectively closed down 602 Squadron on day one by ordering all ranks to be inoculated against typhoid, para typhoid, A & B and cholera. Doc Allan and his orderlies went to work reducing the Squadron to a gang of zombies. I remember the weary figure of my Flight Commander, Marcus Robinson, trudging about his duties dragging his leg across the tarmac. It was just as well Reich Marshal Goering did not get to hear about it. In fact, the German air force were, at that time, fully occupied in Poland, where they are reported to have committed many atrocities.

The absence of enemy activity resulted in a sense of anti climax. The anticipated raids never came - just false alarms. This was just as well. Although we had been provided with one of the best Fighters in the world, Command had managed to render the Spitfire largely ineffective in combat. Air Staff had come to the conclusion that modern aeroplanes were too fast for deflection shooting as practised by the Royal Flying Corps in the Great War. All attacks were to be made from line astern or from astern rising from below. Pilots were ordered to open fire at 400 yards. To make this effective the eight Browning machine guns, spaced along and inside the wings of the Spitfire, were sited and harmonised at 400 yards to produce a spray of bullets corresponding to the rear profile of the fuselage and engine nacelles of a German twin engine bomber, such as the Heinkel 111; with emphasis on the engines. To alter this bullet grouping was to be Court Martial offence.

For aim and range we relied on the reflector sight, an ingenious optical device which produced an image of about a three inch diameter circle appearing just outside the small bullet proof glass panel in front of the pilot's face. The centre of the circle was the aiming point positioned in the middle of a gap between two diametrically opposed visual lines in parallel with the lateral rig of the fighter. This gap could be widened or narrowed by the pilot so as to fit the rear silhouette of the target selected, usually a Heinkel 111 at a range of 400 yards. When the target filled the gap the pilot opened fire.

The sight was perfect but the bullet grouping and the opening range of fire at 400 yards resulted in a dispersal of fire power delivered at too great a distance which, of course, could be further dissipated if the pilot in his anxiety opened fire too soon. Moreover the wings of the target and the fighter had to be exactly parallel otherwise

Fg Off MacLean in his "office". 19 September 1939

any geometric error between them would inevitably cause the bullets to miss. In practice this drawing board perfection was hard to achieve, nor did the Germans co-operate!

The result of this error in tactics was soon demonstrated in the Battle of the Forth on 16th October when 602 and 603 each expended about 18,000 rounds with only two kills over Scotland, although we heard later two more had fallen by the way side across the North Sea to Germany. Like Pharaoh, in the Book of Exodus, Command just hardened its heart and refused to change the orders.

A few days before we moved out under canvas beside "Bessies Farm" on the north-west perimeter of the aerodrome, we were visited in our mess at Abbotsburn House by the Station Commander, Group Captain Jones, father-in-law of Cyril Hodder. He had been an RFC Pilot in the Great War. His message was "If you want to hit anything get in close to it". This seemed to make common sense. "At what range did you open fire, Sir", I asked. "As close as possible" he replied. "Sometimes we used to do it at 5 yards". He made his point. All we could do was smile politely and offer him another glass of sherry.

Soon after we moved out under canvas the summer weather degenerated into autumn with low cloud and fog, which began to ice up on the wings at night. The Spitfires were fitted with HF (High Frequency Radio Telephone) which worked quite well during the daylight hours, but degenerated into a noisy mush after dusk. This, it was said, was due to the "heavy side layer". To cap all this Douglas Farquhar, in what was to prove an impulsive mistake, returned the Squadron as operational by night, which he probably was, but most of us were not.

Most of our night flying in peace time had been deceptively easy with the help of the lights shining in Glasgow, Paisley, Barrhead and other local centres of population. One hardly needed to look at the instruments. Having done one hour in these easy conditions at night in a Spitfire on 17th August I was, I think, theoretically the most experienced night pilot on this type of aeroplane which saved me from an immediate taste of the horrors which faced those whose turn came just after the war was declared, and when the whole of Clydeside was blacked out into pitch darkness. Although beautiful to fly by day the Spitfire by night belched lurid flame and purple sparks from the exhausts on each side of the engine cowling. This fouled up the view ahead, particularly over the port side over which one had to see the ground while landing. To compound our difficulties Command withdrew the landing floodlight leaving only a single sparse line of tiny glim lamps to show the landing strip. Almost at once we lost J M Bryden, a young sergeant pilot who had joined us from the Volunteer Reserve. He took off and went straight in about a mile beyond the end of the runway. After that the corporal in charge of the Link Trainer for blind instrument flying training suddenly found himself very much in business! There were other incidents. Command had recognised our status as a night flying squadron, so there was no going back on this decision which landed 602 for many months with the whole air night defence of Scotland. 603 Squadron was only just converting to Spitfires, nor was there any relief for us when crack regular squadrons, such as 72 and 111, joined us at Drem. They were, as yet, unqualified to operate at night, but were probably just as well if not better trained in night flying than we were. Seen in retrospect it is now clear that Senior Regular Commanders, such as Harry Broadhurst of 111 Squadron, must have realised that night patrols in Spitfires and Hurricanes could be a dangerous waste of pilots and aircraft. They obviously stuck in their toes as we should have done.

But all this was still to come. Douglas did what he could to deal with the situation. By this time the headlights on all motor cars were cleverly shielded by covers which allowed light through a narrow slit shaped rather like a Croix de Loraine. George Pinkerton, who had a fine set of headlights, lent his motor car with the blackout shields temporarily removed.

The car was driven out on to the aerodrome to replace the floodlight. The extra illumination just made the difference provided one managed to touch down within the beam which would be switched on just in time for the landing. My turn soon came. Fortified by a couple of visits to the Link Trainer I charged up into the blackout. The heavy side layer had taken over the RT. Fighter Control at Turnhouse could do nothing if you got lost. While stooging around, it became increasingly obvious that the odds on finding and destroying an enemy aircraft without search lights were about the same as swotting a fly in a bedroom with the lights turned off. I remembered with some amusement the comments of an elderly Flight Lieutenant in 269 Squadron at Abbotsinch when he declared "the night was made for better things"!

Finding my way back to Abbotsinch down I came but, despite the assistance of George's headlights, dropped my Spitfire on the ground from about some six feet with a sickening crunch in full view of Douglas who was so shaken by the sight that he sent me on 24 hours leave. I was later somewhat comforted to learn that George Pinkerton, one of our most experienced pilots, had broken his aircraft landing.

Sooner or later there had to be a night flap. By the grace of God first off was Sandy Johnstone, our most experienced "Night 'Awk". He had been an instructor in navigation with many hours night flying for David MacIntyre at Prestwick. Off he went through the foggy darkness. He could see nothing. It was in fact just another false alarm. Denied a fix from control on the RT because of the heavy side layer, Sandy soon lost himself. Realising his number was up, he descended to a safe height and with great presence of mind pulled off a parachute flare. There right below him was a lovely aerodrome which he had never noticed before during several years flying round the district. Just before he touched down he realised to his horror that it was a reservoir! With a burst of throttle he crossed the water and pancaked on a hillside. There he was soon greeted by a very suspicious farmer armed with a shot gun. Having convinced the man he was not a German, Sandy was welcomed into the farmhouse and put to bed. This brilliant but unnecessary feat of airmanship did little to encourage our morale. My own craven reaction was "Thank God it wasn't my turn!"

It was just as well that none of this was known to the Luftwaffe. Fortunately they were still busy in Poland. It is interesting to speculate what might have happened if they had sent a few unarmed bombers, under the command of experienced Luftwaffe pilots, to stooge around above the rain and fog in Scotland, drawing up the best of our fighter pilots and exposing them to the sort of hazards from which Sandy was very lucky to escape. He could so easily have ploughed into a dyke. In Sandy's case there was no need for German co-operation, it was just a friendly bomber which had become lost.

Meantime the phoney war continued. Even Group, no doubt prompted by Douglas, realised that Abbotsinch was a non starter. By October we began to land our patrols at Grangemouth, a huge airfield now occupied by an Oil Refinery.

On 6th October 'A' Flight landed off patrol at Grangemouth, and there we remained, joined later by 'B' Flight. Grangemouth was just a club house with no where to sleep. Douglas and Ding Dong went to work. When dusk fell a van ferried the weary pilots to a strange old fashioned looking villa in Falkirk which looked respectable outside, but had a curious smell inside. We were well looked after by the occupants. These were a number of young but kindly females. It did not dawn on me at the time, but I am inclined to think it may have been a brothel. Of course, we all know that there never was, and never could be, such a place in Falkirk; but it appeals to my rather warped sense of fun that Douglas could be the only CO in the RAF to billet his boys in a brothel.

Despite a good nights rest in Falkirk I developed tooth ache. Ding Dong was splendid. After ferreting out the appropriate rules he produced a form which demanded a diagnosis. "Careys" he suggested, so we settled for that. I set off on foot to a dentist in Grangemouth. He did a good job for which I hope he charged the Air Ministry his fee of five shillings. Just as well because for me that was nearly half a day's pay saved.

We shared Grangemouth with 603 who were using it to convert their pilots to Spitfires. Regrettably they had a fatal accident when one of their pilots who had just landed was chewed up in his cockpit by a prop of another learner who had landed directly behind him. This was always a danger with Spitfires because once you were down, the nose with its long Merlin engine rose so high that nothing could be seen dead ahead.

Grangemouth was not to last. Group must have had their eye on Drem which was the obvious base for the defence of the West of Scotland from air attack across the North Sea. One evening early in October Douglas ordered me to fly to Drem next morning and have breakfast there. "Watch your landing" he said, "there's a damp strip on the south side of the aerodrome". "When you get back report on the condition of the grass aerodrome for landing. Don't go on your nose". Good advice because that was the most common form of accident.

Realising I was flying in the role of a guinea pig, I had a good look down at Drem which was sited on a hill side with a slope down from north to south. As usual the wind was from the south-west which meant landing down hill. There was indeed a lush green strip at the foot right across the south side of the aerodrome. The angle of the slope did not look much less than my gliding angle so what would happen when I reached the green strip. Having landed successfully, I taxied cautiously out the soft ground, and then off to join the Flying Training School officers at breakfast in their comfortable and well appointed Mess. I became the subject of suspicious glances. I think they suspected my presence as the writing on the wall recorded by Daniel at Belshazzars Feast. Indeed it was!

"It can be done with care" I reported to Douglas on return to Grangemouth. The Squadron took off for Drem the next morning and a few days later the Flying Training School went off to Montrose.

I have always been intrigued by my selection for this operation. Harking back to those tedious little sums we did at school. Was I the Squadron's lowest common multiple (our LCM) or was I the highest common factor (the Squadron's HCF). Put another way - if Hector could do it who couldn't!

When the troops arrived all the accommodation at Drem was already occupied by the Training School airmen so our men had to be billeted temporarily in the Marine Hotel, Gullane, which had been commandeered with admirable speed by the Station Commander, Group Captain Charles Keary.

That evening Douglas went up to Gullane to inspect the new quarters and found the Marine Hotel blazing with light from all its windows. "I shall come back tomorrow armed with a revolver" he said, "and I shall fire it through any window showing light". The following evening when darkness fell Douglas and Ding Dong went again to Gullane. Not a chink of light could be seen, so in they went to congratulate the troops. To their surprise they found no carpets. It was not long before the penny dropped, they had been cut up and nailed over the windows. The troops had won!

The Squadron thereafter resumed the defence of Scotland against air attack which was shared by day with 603 who were rapidly becoming operational on their Spitfires. 602 was stuck with all the night readiness. I do not think the RAF had any night fighters at this stage in the war, but I may be wrong about that because there were Blenheim Squadrons down south. Without ground control and air born radar the state of the art rendered night patrolling without search lights; a more or less useless exercise. However, it enabled the newspapers to boast that our fighters had gone up. As no German ever came down this did not add to our popularity. There was, however, the chance of getting the odd enemy reconnaissance aircraft by day, if and when it really turned out to be a Hun.

Air Chief Marshal Dowding's control and reporting system (C & R) was magnificently conceived, but was suffering from teething troubles and limitations which only experience could cure. This resulted in considerable frustration and wasted engine hours.

The C & R organisation was so secret that initially the pilots were only allowed to know what was good for them; and that wasn't much. The lid has now been off for so many years there are few secrets left, if any. Without a brief description of the C & R system it could be difficult for the modern reader to understand the sort of problems which faced Fighter Command and the Squadrons during those early war years.

Initially there were four Fighter Groups. Ten Group in the south-west of England with headquarters near Bath, Eleven Group in the south-east of England including London based at Uxbridge, Twelve Group at Hucknall near Nottingham for the Midlands, and Thirteen Group at Ouston near Newcastle-on-Tyne which was supposed to cover the whole of Scotland and the North of England. At a later stage 9 Group, with its Headquarters near Preston, assumed responsibility for the western side of Britain, north of the 10 Group area. The Group areas were sub divided into sectors each of which had a Sector Commander with an operations room from which his fighters were controlled by RT. Fighter Command operated from a deep hole lined with concrete at Bentley Priory near Stanmore from which they exercised overall control over the Groups. Each Group had its own operations room with a large plotting table covering their sectors with a margin of overlap. The plotting table at Bentley Priory covered the whole of Britain.

The map was divided into 50 mile squares with each square subdivided into five mile squares. This was known as the Fighter Command Grid which made plotting possible.

The fighters were initially ordered up by the Group Controller who was a Wing Commander. Thereafter they were handled by the Sector Controller using RT. The position of his fighters was ascertained by means of a device in the aircraft known as a "pip squeak" which emitted a signal at regular intervals during each minute. These noises were received by two or three Direction Finding (DF) stations, widely spread geographically around the sector area.

The DF radio operator at each station would phone in the bearing to his opposite number who was a plotter armed with a string sitting at a map of the sector on a small separate plotting table. Where the strings crossed there would be the fighters, or rather where they had been a number of seconds before. The Fighter Command grid co-ordinates of the fighter formation would then be told by telephone to the plotters at the Group and Sector Operations tables. The pipsqueak was soon superseded by plain voice fixing and dead reckoning in the Ops room done by a sergeant deputy controller.

Plotting and identifying the enemy was much more difficult. Each Group had a Filter Room with telephone lines to the Royal Observer Corps (ROC) centres and radar stations in its area. Each of these information sources was linked by telephone to a plotter (usually a WAAF) at the filtering table. She would be armed with an array of symbols, such as Halma men and specially shaped tiddly winks. Each symbol spoke its own message such as the number of aircraft, the range, the height and direction.

The Filtering Officer would then read the signs and put down a plot indicating the position, number, height and direction of the aircraft; but not as yet identified. That was then the problem. This they strove to solve by means of the Movement Liaison Service (the MLS).

The whole of the North Sea was reserved for the war as a no-go area. All friendly aircraft had to clear with the MLS, so in theory any unexpected plot over the sea had to be hostile. The Royal Observer Corps were supposed to report and identify all aircraft movements over land. With a plot on his table the Filter Controller would take advice from his MLO and allot an identification. 'H' for hostile, 'X' for unidentified bogies, and 'F' for friendly; and that is how it would be told by telephone to the Fighter Operations rooms. It all sounded so simple, but in practice the radar stations were weak on height, and the Observer Corps could not see at night, or through clouds by day. The friendly movements when notified did not always coincide with their flight plans, and there were other technical limitations in the radar equipment.

The time lags differed between the various sources of information gathered in this secret background. With an 'H' or an 'X' raid on the Group operations table we would be scrambled off the ground by Sector Control all steamed up to do battle, only to find an Anson or a Hudson returning to Leuchars!

Much more frustrating was an 'Ogo Pogo' patrol; caused by a mythical (bird) begotten by the C & R organisation and which existed in the imagination of the fighter pilot. The bird infested the North Sea and was wont to fly in circles of ever decreasing radius until it finally flew up its own fundamental orifice; and then from that impregnable position it would hurl back its own excreta at its baffled adversaries! More technical information is needed to explain the environment in which the Ogo Pogo thrived.

Although we were not initially told about this, the CH station coverage extended in a floodlight beam about 150 miles out over the sea in the elevated profile of a huge pear. Its coverage was, therefore, comparatively low near the coast but then rose to about 25,000 feet at its extremity. I have made rough sketches of the radar coverage as I remember it. These may help to explain the foregoing description. The CH station was accurate on range but the position and height of an aircraft could not be estimated unless the filter room got a range cut from two CH stations. Height finding was complicated and inaccurate, nor was there any cover against low flying raiders until the new Chain Home Low (CHL) stations were installed much later on suitable cliff tops. The whole process was bedevilled by differing time lags.

Approaching high in the sky the enemy would frequently disappear from the CH beams as he approached the coast. Alternatively he would come in low enough to avoid detection all together, which he did when attacking our coastal shipping.

Working with these rudimentary tools, and after a time lag of say one minute, the filter room would identify and tell through a hostile. Then after a further delay of, say, one minute, the Group Controller would issue his orders to the Sector Controller. Then after another, say, three to five minutes off would go the readiness section of three fighters from Turnhouse or Drem, climbing at normal speed. As the hostile or bogey approached the coast it would fade above the narrowing radar lobe and disappear from the ops room table. "I must get them there quickly" thinks the Sector Controller and orders "Buster" speed. No sooner done then the enemy reappears on the table going into reverse, back to Germany, but it is the fighters the radar stations are now reporting. The penny drops in the Ops Room for the unfortunate Controller. The fighters are off in the wrong direction. He orders them on to a reciprocal course. "Gate" (all out) "for Dunbar" he orders, and so the Ogo Pogo wins again. The wily Hun was either in a cloud or never was there in the first place. Perhaps a bit later a lucky Hudson might land back at Leuchars.

The truth of the matter is that the system was designed to deal with easily detected mass raids for which it worked well. Sneak raiders and reconnaissance hostiles were much more difficult to find, although we managed to bag a few.

Each flight had two sections of three aircraft. Red and yellow sections for 'A' Flight, and Blue and Green for 'B' Flight. There were five states of readiness:- "Stand-by" which meant sitting in the aircraft strapped in without the engine running; "Readiness" meaning able to take off within five minutes; "Fifteen Minutes" available and "Thirty Minutes" available and "Released". The Readiness section could be brought to "Stand By" with the pilots strapped into their seats in the aircraft, the starter battery trolleys plugged into the engines, and the pilot's helmets plugged into their radio and oxygen tubes, but you could not start the engine for fear of over heating. The Merlin engine, as fitted to the Spitfire, was cooled by an airflow through a small external scoop under the fuselage. Without air flow on the ground the radiator did not function properly with the result that once the engine was started heat began to build up quite rapidly. In consequence the pilot had to get off the ground in fairly quick time or abandon the flight. If he left it too late the engine could seize up during take off.

Incidents such as the Ogo Pogo and other false alarms had undermined my confidence in the ability of sector control to identify enemy targets. This was weighing heavily on my mind when the balloon went up on 16th October 1939. On that morning the Squadron had been hunting an enemy reconnaissance raid without success. It probably was a reconnaissance flight because about 1.30 p.m. A Flight was suddenly ordered to patrol Turnhouse. As we climbed to the east the sky above Edinburgh was filling up with dirty looking little black smudges. Odd looking balloons I thought. Then the penny dropped. "Good heavens they must be AA bursts". Nothing came from Control but there seemed to be some turmoil over the Forth Bridge. We dived down and there I saw three twin engined aeroplanes flying east. I approached them looking for swastikas and found none, but hold it there were black crosses instead. I had wasted valuable seconds. The enemy '88s were going at full throttle and I could hardly catch them. Away along the Fife coast I got in range, just as I was closing in another Spitfire (from 603 I think) swooped in behind the enemy a few feet from my starboard wing tip. He was banked to starboard so obviously had not seen me. The Germans nearly got us both it was such a near miss - another of my nine lives gone!

When the other Spitfire had broken off I moved in and gave them all I had but apparently did no better than the 603 man unless, of course, it was one of the two 88s that fell on the way home. Back I went at once to rearm in case of a follow-up raid cursing my naive and slow reactions.

Douglas, with Sandy and Ian Ferguson, had run low on petrol hunting the reconnaissance aircraft. They landed to refuel at Leuchars where they hoped to get lunch ,when the Ju88s were seen. At first they thought they were Blenheims, but then a few minutes later realised they were Ju88s so dashed out to their aircraft to take off, which they did to the accompaniment of ribald cheering from the Coastal Command ground crews and the displeasure of Group Captain Baker, disgusted not only with Fighter Command, but with his luncheon guests.

While Douglas, Sandy and Ian were crossing the Firth they were mistaken for enemy

Chain Home (CH) Floodlight Beams

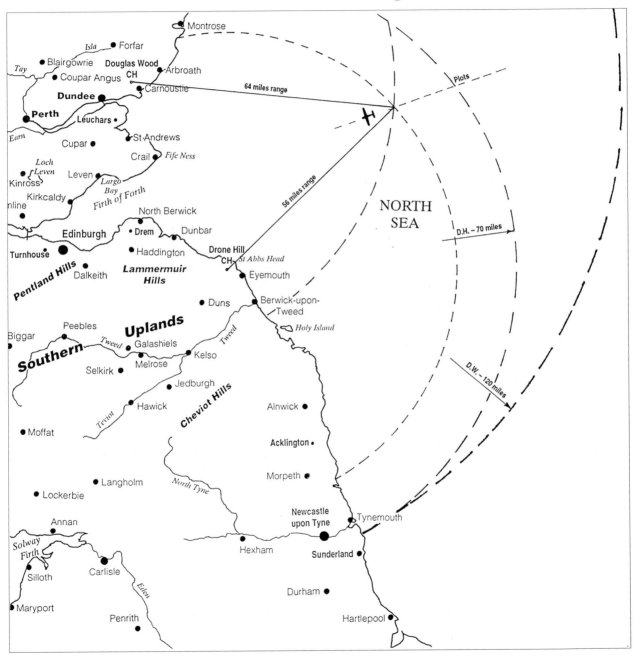

Memory of Chain Home Radar (CH)

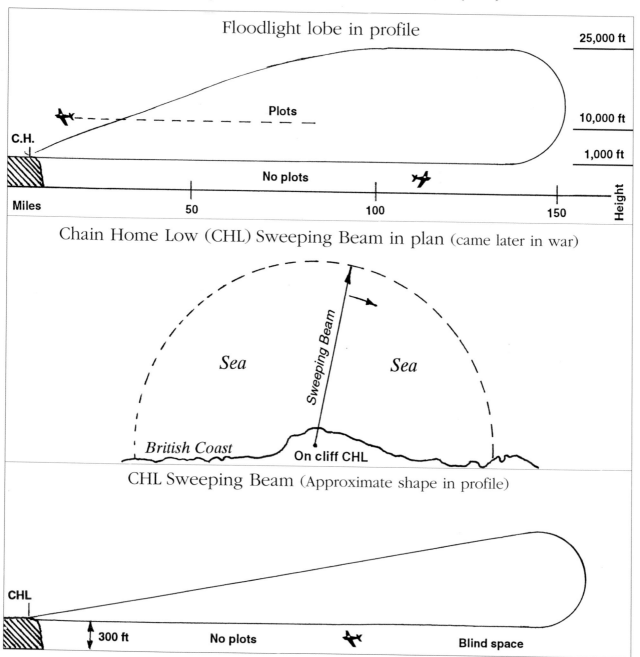

Floodlight lobe in profile

25,000 ft

10,000 ft

1,000 ft

Plots

C.H.

No plots

Miles   50   100   150   Height

Chain Home Low (CHL) Sweeping Beam in plan (came later in war)

Sea   Sea

Sweeping Beam

British Coast

On cliff CHL

CHL Sweeping Beam (Approximate shape in profile)

CHL

300 ft   No plots   Blind space

aircraft and fired on by the carrier Furious which was zig-zagging up and down the river at high speed to avoid becoming a casualty. Fortunately George Pinkerton and Archie McKellar brought one of the enemy aircraft down. Patsy Gifford of 603 got the other - both Ju88s.

There followed the usual nonsense in the newspapers and elsewhere as to which Squadron had downed the first German over Britain. Glasgow and Edinburgh again - but who cares. The raid on Rosyth was hailed by the press as a victory. Heroic air born lawyers, rhubarb growers and sheep farmers were the talk of the town! Lord Haw Haw on the German/English radio service also claimed success, and may have been nearer the truth because the Luftwaffe had, in fact, landed a bomb on one of our cruisers at Rosyth. The raid was not as commonly supposed, aimed at the Forth Bridge. Despite their success the

Flt Lt George Pinkerton   *Fg Off Archie McKellar*

Drawings by Cuthbert Orde

76

German air force must have got quite a shock by the scale of the defence and the apparent ability of Fighter Command to get its fighters into action. For them this also meant there must have been a proper system of warning about which, at that time, they were still in a state of ignorance. We did get some satisfaction when we heard that the German air force had nicknamed the Firth of Forth as "suicide alley".

According to Sandy in his book the German casualties were, in fact, four Ju88s and a reconnaissance Heinkel which came to grief in the sea off the Lothian coast. As a result of the Forth raid Fighter Command were apparently persuaded that Scotland required stronger air defences. 72 Squadron in Gladiators had already arrived with Ronnie Lees, an Australian, as their Commanding Officer. They were soon in action. In addition 111 Squadron arrived at Drem with their Hurricanes under the command of Harry Broadhurst, already regarded as an outstanding leader. The enemy must soon have got the message. No more raids on "suicide alley". Nothing was left for these eager

Hector MacLean at Drem
October 1939

beavers but a meagre diet of sneak raiders engaged on reconnaissance or attacking coastal shipping and even fishing boats. It must have been dangerous work in clear weather because the Drem Squadrons bagged quite a few of them. We had our share.

December 21st 1939 was a disaster. Late that day, about fourteen Handley Page Hampden bombers were returning at low level from a raid over Germany to a temporary base in the Moray Firth. With their navigation about 100 miles adrift they hit the Scottish coast somewhere between St Abbs Head and Dunbar. Whether they knew their position we were never told. One thing for sure the Squadron Leader in command cannot have known he was heading into a hornets nest, otherwise he would surely have ordered his boys to drop their wheels which was the appropriate sign of non military intentions. Arriving all the way below radar cover they were unplotted and unexpected in the Turnhouse Sector Ops Room.

No warning came from 13 Group or from Fighter Command. Accordingly they were plotted as hostile.

602 were the Duty Squadron at Drem. A sudden message came on the station tannoy. "All Squadrons scramble - Hostiles approaching". There were no runways. Spitfires took off straight from their dispersal points in all directions. Fortunately my section yellow was not first off. The sun was going down behind North Berwick Law and visibility degenerating into a foggy twilight. Suddenly there was the enemy just east of the town. "Tally ho". But hold it. I was lucky; the setting sun revealed a surprising silouhette. "My God they are flying suitcases". For that is what the Hampdens were so aptly named. Despite looking like a suitcase from the side the Hampden viewed from astern looked like most other twin engine aeroplanes. Some of our pilots who got there a bit earlier and who made contact from astern had no reason to doubt they were hostile as announced by the Controller, so in they went. I saw what was happening and shouted through the RT. "They're Hampdens" but no one heard. Two of the bombers came down in the sea. Most of the crew survived but one of them was drowned in Aberlady Bay.

Air Chief Marshal Sir Richard Pierce, Commander in Chief Bomber Command came up for the Enquiry. The Squadron must have been exonerated. Certainly no one was punished. The bomber boys took it badly and who could blame them. We watched in sad disgrace as they took off to their home base at Waddington, streaming lavatory paper across Drem aerodrome.

November 14th was for me a hairy day. In response to a request from his opposite number Finlay Crerar, the CO of 612 Squadron, who needed an officer to conduct an investigation, Douglas despatched me in my Spitfire to Dyce near Aberdeen. I landed cross wind into a sea of mud and then roared my way across the aerodrome unsticking myself at almost full throttle and my tail rising up dangerously. By the time I reached the watch office the engine temperature was at danger. On reporting to Squadron Leader Crerar I told him as politely as I could what I thought of his aerodrome for Spitfires, but he failed to register. Taxiing Ansons through mud was a very different cup of tea. My real worry was whether I had made myself a prisoner in the mud at Dyce. Fortunately by the time the investigation was complete and the report made, my engine had cooled, and so back through the mud to the take off point with the needle almost at danger. I had had enough of Dyce so decided to give it a go. I was lucky. Under full power I gained enough speed and lift to take the weight off the wheels and so staggered into the cooling air with the aid of my faithful Merlin engine which smelt as though it was red hot. 'E' for Edward had done well to restart without the assistance of a starting battery – not provided by RAF Dyce.

On 8th February 1940 Douglas ordered me to fly to Leuchars where I would be contacted by Dundee University boffins working at Douglas Wood CH station, with a view to air testing some new radar equipment.

One weakness of the Chain Home radar direction finding system (later in the war referred to as "Steam Radar") was its inability to distinguish, and so report, our own aircraft. The boffins had come up with a device known as IFF (Identification Friend from Foe). I was to have the experimental equipment fitted to 'E' for Edward, my aeroplane. On February 8th I ran into thick fog at Fife Ness which was down on the sea at St Andrews so I had to try again next day. On arrival I parked 'E' beside the watch office and phoned the boffins. They soon arrived. "You will have to leave the aeroplane here," they said. "We need 3 days to fit the equipment". This suited me fine, so off I went on a 48 hour self granted leave of absence to visit Marcia Dods the lady who became my first wife. I arrived at Dulnain Bridge, but only just, after a hair-raising drive through the snow on the A9 road. When I got back to Leuchars 'E' for Edward had disappeared. "Are you MacLean?" "Yes". "Where the hell have you been? The Navy have reported a Spitfire diving into the Firth of Forth. Your Squadron have been out searching for your remains." "What have you done with my aeroplane" I replied with considerable irritation. "What aeroplane?" they asked. "The aeroplane I am supposed to be sitting in at the bottom of the Firth of Forth" I replied. The Corporal of the Watch denied all knowledge of a Spitfire. Finally I found 'E' in the middle of Leuchars Aerodrome, admittedly almost hull down as viewed from the watch office window. The boffins had moved it there to avoid radio interference but they had not bothered to tell anyone. Moreover they were not even ready, and continued to tinker with 'E' for another two days. When I phoned Douglas he sounded quite relieved and made some caustic remark about the Navy being unable to distinguish a Spitfire from a seagull! He was probably right. At this early stage of the war the Royal Navy betrayed no interest in, and cared less, about aircraft recognition. They just blazed away at any aircraft within range. Two years later in Northern Ireland it was just the same.

The object of the IFF was to cause the fighter's blip on the CH radar screen to jerk itself in rather a suggestive obscene manner. The RAF never missed a trick. It was soon nicknamed the "Cockerel". I did the trial flights on the 15th and 16th February over the North Sea without VHF which had been replaced by the experimental equipment. It was not very impressive because I had to keep twiddling a knob to make it work. However, the boffins were satisfied and in due course the IFF "cockerels" were pulsing from our Spitfires in the radar stations automatically, and without any assistance from the pilot. I heard later that we had given this vital equipment to the French, who let it fall into German hands.

My brief return flight from Leuchars to Drem nearly ended in disaster. On taxiing up to the dispersal smoke was pouring out of the radio compartment. When reinstalling my wireless set the brilliant boffins had crossed up the wires. According to Sergeant Nicol, our wireless expert, another two minutes in the air would have seen me off in flames. Perhaps another of my nine lives gone!

On 22nd December Red Sector led by Dunlop Urie with "Fumff" Strong and myself destroyed a Heinkel 111. Our additional speed got us there before the Hurricanes of 111 Squadron, and just before it could escape into cloud. A row developed with Harry Broadhurst who accused 'A' Flight of poaching!

On January 13th A Flight, led by Marcus Robinson, destroyed a Heinkel 111 near May Island. I came in second or third but the tail gunner was still alive because he put a bullet through my canopy with a piece of perspex in my eye so I decided not to wait to witness the end of our victim.

Despite the Hampden debacle we continued to enjoy the confidence of Fighter Command who sent us George Proudman, a superb pilot from 65 Squadron. He brought his Spitfire fitted with an experimental cannon fitted in each wing. He was attended by a Squadron Leader from the Armaments Branch to supervise the testing of this new development. George spent each and every day with our readiness sections in the hope that we would find and lead him in, as and when the enemy were prepared to offer him suitable prey for his cannons. Douglas was keen to get in on the act and liked to lead the cannon. The opportunity came on 22nd February 1940 when they intercepted a Heinkel 111 over the sea off St Abbs Head. Douglas went in first in case the canons did not work. He silenced the rear gunner and in went George Proudman, but his cannons only fired a few rounds and then stopped. The bomber came down on the moor near Coldingham. As some of Proudman's shells might have struck home Douglas was keen to preserve the evidence before the Germans set fire to their aircaraft, so down he went and attempted a landing on the moor beside the wrecked bomber – going upside down and becoming trapped in his cockpit, from which ignominious position the Heinkel crew managed to rescue him!

It is hard to believe Douglas really thought he could land in such a place. Spitfires were badly needed and in short supply. He obviously got away with it because he was soon promoted to Wing Commander, given the DFC and posted away to be a Station Commander.

Before leaving Drem Douglas and Harry Broadhurst ganged up to have the guns of 602 and 111 focused at a point of 250 yards ahead. The same message was, I believe, coming from the Hurricane pilots in the British Expeditionary Force (the BEF) in Belgium. Command appears to have acquiesced. After that we really began to get results.

The cannons had obviously failed their test in action, so George Proudman and his Squadron Leader were withdrawn for modifications. In due course they returned with the cannons in much better working order, and we had the benefit of George's company for a good spell. He used to fly No 2 in my section. I would turn my head to see him tucked in behind my starboard wing tip, flying upside down and smoking a pipe! We were sorry to see him leave again for 65 Squadron, and shocked to hear that he had been killed, I think, over Dunkirk. He was reported to have performed upward rolls through the centre of the defensive circle formed by the German twin engined Messerschmitt 110s when under attack. He was too good to last.

On a date I cannot remember I had the misfortune to break a wing tip. There had been a flap at Drem with sections taking off in a late foggy afternoon. It had been an attack on a CH Station; but it was over and we were ordered to land. I began the turn back to Drem and was pumping down the undercarriage. Just before the final stroke on the black lever a section of Hurricanes came streaking out of the foggy air straight at us. I pulled back the stick and by the mercy of God they passed just below. As the adrenaline gradually settled I brought the section back to Drem and duly landed kissing the turf in style; but suddenly the starboard wing began to drop. Oh my God, I had forgotten to complete the last pump stroke. One wheel was almost, but not quite down. The wing sank to the ground and round went 'E' for Edward to an ignominious halt. It was quite infuriating because I was one of the very few, if not the only pilot, who had not broken a Spitfire. Worse still the news filtered through to Group where the Mills of God began to grind. Meanwhile 'E' for Edward was soon back on the job with a new wing tip.

Early in 1940 George Pinkerton was promoted to Squadron Leader and posted to command No.65 Squadron at Hornchurch. J D Urie had taken over 'A' Flight on the departure of Marcus Robinson to command No.616 at Leconfield.

We had previously been joined by Flying Officer P J Strong, a regular officer who had just returned from a tour of duty with the a squadron in Egypt, bringing with him a ribald sense of humour and a loud voice. He also brought with him his wife, and installed her in Bissets Hotel, Gullane. "Come up to Bissets and meet the old bag" was his invitation. With some hesitation two of us went up to Bissets Hotel to be greeted by a stunning blonde built to beautiful and generous specifications!

Strong was known as "Fumff" because his voice resembled a radio character employed, I think, by the BBC to make fun of Lord Haw Haw. Although he enjoyed obvious home comforts Fumff was a keen student of female form and studied all the available pornography. When he found a picture to his taste he would suggest that all she needed was one of Uncle Strong's hot meat injections! Despite these dubious abhorations Fumff, by reason of his regular training, knew all the ropes including the organisation of service funerals with airmen firing off rifle volleys. We only once needed his services.

I last remember "Fumff" flying as a No 3 in Red Section led by Dunlop near St Abbs. We intercepted a Ju88 at about 20,000 feet which immediately went into almost vertical power dive. Dunlop managed to catch up and fire his guns with the 88 gathering speed every second. I came next. When all my rounds were gone I noticed with alarm that the needle on the air speed indicator had gone round about twice. My speed was probably well over 500 miles per hour. Time to pull out, but would the wings take it in time. The 88 still nearly vertical had disappeared into a cloud about 5,000 feet. I emerged below with a few hundred feet to spare. No sign of the enemy except a large circular patch of frothing water on the surface of the sea. Fumff who was an experienced pilot survived, so presumably had the sense to pull out sooner or would have suffered the same fate as the unfortunate Ju88.

March 2nd remains a vivid memory. Two or three of us had taken off on night flying practice during which control suddenly announced that there were hostiles attacking ships off St Abbs Head. Here at last was a chance to catch them at it while we were airbourn. With a half moon to help it would be possible to take one's eyes off the instruments and concentrate on searching. We raced for St Abbs but no trace of the enemy and no burning ships down below. Perhaps they were still lurking about so I turned on my navigation lights as a ruse which might trick them into shooting and so give themselves away. Either they did not fall for it or had gone home. In retrospect just as well! The patrol had lasted an hour and a half. I landed back absolutely exhausted. Douglas was quite impressed and offered me a cigarette. It was one of the few I have ever smoked and I found it remarkably soothing.

Douglas Farquhar departed about the end of March 1940 and was succeeded by George Pinkerton, by which time I was in trouble over that wretched wing tip. Would I take a Court

Martial or elect to be dealt with by the AOC? In due course I appeared before the Air Vice Marshal Birdie Saul. "Any more trouble from you MacLean" he said "and I will send you to Bomber Command". I was speechless and luckily restrained myself from asking him whether Bomber Command, for whom I had enormous admiration, would take his throw outs.

The Filter Room
RAF Fighter Command, Bentley Priory

CHAPTER 8
DREM/MONTROSE/DYCE

During February and March 1940 the Squadron was mainly occupied with convoy and coastal shipping protection in the North Sea. Merchant ships accumulated in Methil Bay over which we frequently had to maintain a standing patrol of one or sometimes two aircraft. It was dull work and heavy on engine hours, but the word must have got back to Germany because I do not think any attacks were ever attempted - just snoopers.

By the beginning of April 603 Squadron had a Flight based at Montrose from which they maintained a standing patrol over the sea between Dundee and Aberdeen. They soon began to run out of engine hours, and so on 4th April I was sent over from Drem to reinforce them with the mighty 'E' for Edward, the slowest aeroplane in 602.

It was the first visit to Montrose by air by a member of the MacLean family since 1913. The Royal Flying Corps (RFC) came into existence in 1912. Montrose, probably the first aerodrome in Scotland, was in operation before the spring of 1913. No 2 Squadron equipped with BE2s was based there, midway between the naval base at Rosyth and Scapa Flow. My uncle, then Lieutenant A C H MacLean seconded from the Royal Scots to the RFC, landed there early in 1913 and reported to Captain Longcroft, OC 'B' Flight, who asked him why he had come. "To fly the BE2" was my Uncle Campbell's reply. But would he be any good thought Longcroft; so he took out a cigarette and asked Campbell for a light and observed his hand. "You have a steady hand MacLean" he observed, "I expect you will do". This remark still rang true for me in 1940 because one did indeed require a steady hand to cope with a sudden loss of air speed when your aeroplane passed over the dunes as it approached from the sea. It was, I think, caused by the west wind rising over the dunes leaving a patch of calm air below just in the touchdown area inside the aerodrome. Although I approached with a good margin of flying speed the Spitfire dropped out of my hands onto the grass just beyond the dunes. Fortunately the undercarriage took it so I taxied in rather sheepishly to the 603 dispersal, which looked rather like a poor relation at the north end of the aerodrome. Either 603 did not notice or they were once more too polite to comment! It turned out they did not really want me; but they needed 'E' for Edward having run out of engine hours on their North Sea operation, named Viken Zero. The object was to catch the wily Heinkels and

Ju88s who had been sneaking in under the radar cover to bomb and strafe merchant ships and fishing boats, and even light houses. This did not improve their reputation on the East Coast of Scotland, but in spite of that I had to admit a grudging respect for the German air crews engaged on this work. They were hard to find but when we did they would be outnumbered, outpaced and out gunned. Without handy cloud cover they were doomed. In August the situation would be reversed. We would be up against German fighters, not just bombers, and we would be heavily outnumbered. The enemy must soon have got wind of 603 at Dyce and Montrose because they became fewer and hard to catch.

Flight Lieutenant "Rusty" Rushmer, a courteous and efficient auxiliary officer was in

603 Squadron 'B' Flight at Montrose, July 1940
Standing – Cpl Brand; Cp Cantley; F/Sgt Mackie; Sgt Gillies; Sgt Sanderson; Cpl Murray
Seated – Plt Off Berry; Flt Lt Rushmer; Plt Off Benson

command of the detachment. Sadly he was to be killed later in the Battle of Britain. He allowed me four patrols before I was ordered back to Drem on 10th April, by which time Hitler had invaded Norway.

My stay with 603 may have coincided with the arrival of Richard Hillary, the author of "The Last Enemy" who was appointed to Rusty's Flight. The book contains a vivid description of the 603 detachment and the dispersal point at the north end of Montrose aerodrome. 'A' Flight 602 replaced them on the 14th April under the command of John Dunlop Urie.

The battles in Norway were raging apace, but we saw nothing of them except an increasing number of false alarms resulting in the interception of Coastal Command aircraft. Inevitably someone clobbered an Anson - fortunately none of 'A' Flight's doing. We were now under control from Dyce, near Aberdeen, which had a temporary control room.

At this point I cannot resist telling Sandy Johnstone's story of Archie at the Fighter Control operations room at Dyce as it was coming into existence. They were inundated with joiners, carpenters, painters, and a veritable army of post office engineers. Owing to the shortage of telephone switch boards 'B' Flight had to make do with individual telephones, and at one time were the proud possessors of no fewer than twenty-three such instruments, all alike and placed along the newly constructed dais.

This was fine and looked very imposing until one of them rang. Then it was sheer pandemonium trying to find out which one it was. If two rang together they just gave up. By the time half the hand pieces had been replaced on the wrong bases due to the haste the caller had given up and rung off.

There was one telephone they could not fathom. This was the 23rd in line and was set a little apart from the others. Many times in an effort to discover to where the instrument was connected they turned the small handle and got no reply. After it had been lying in its aloof and rather lonely position for more than three weeks it suddenly burst forth - ringing shrilly.

Archie McKellar happened to be nearby and picked up the receiver while they all crowded round eager to hear the voice of the mystery caller. "This is the AOC", said the voice in a distant voice, just loud enough for most of them to hear as they looked over Archieís shoulder. "Oh yes" replied Archie, "Well this is the King of Siam here, how do you do". For a second or two there was silence, and the sound of someone taking a deep breath. Then came an angry shout "Damn it you young whippersnapper - who are you anyway, do you realise who you are talking to".

"I am sorry I could not quite catch that," said Archie quietly. This time the silence was even longer, then the voice came through once more. It was by now calm and collected and speaking very deliberately so that no one could possibly make any mistakes. "This is Air Vice Marshal R E Saul - can you understand that. Now do you know to whom you are speaking". Quick as a flash Archie muttered in the affirmative and added, "Do you know to whom you are speaking". "No". "Thank goodness for that" replied Archie as he hastily replaced the receiver. There was a rueful smile on his face, "That must be a direct line to the AOC - imagine that; what a hell of a way to find out".

When Air Vice Marshal Saul next visited us they explained in full what had happened, and he laughed just as much as 'B' Flight had done over their frightful mistake.

The Viken Zero standing patrols continued unabated from Montrose. In the pilot's hut we were connected with Dyce by a special operational line which terminated on a small plate with a little black flap. This would fall down with a buzz if the Control Room required

Spitfire Is, L1002 'LO-D' (Urie's aircraft) and L1040 'LO-E' (MacLean's aircraft) prepare to take off from Drem in March 1940

our services. In filthy weather we would sit in the hut at night at readiness watching the flap which used to quiver behind a catch before it fell. Frequently it only just quivered but did not fall. Sighs of relief, but we were sorely tempted to file a groove under that catch. Chewing gum would have been too obvious!

By day we spent much time on endless games of Ludo at a shilling a corner. There was a picture of us in the newspapers, including myself, whiling away our time at Drem earnestly engaged in a game of Chess. Don't believe it. This picture was posed on the spur of the moment to give the press some action for their cameras. Perhaps the Ludo board was lost or left at Montrose together with the special metal Ludo lozenges our ingenious airmen had cut and painted, to keep their young masters quiet and out of mischief! Meanwhile at Montrose Findlay Boyd reigned supreme as Ludo champion. I cannot remember how he came to be there. 'B' Flight must have had aircraft at Montrose from time to time. Findlay certainly never failed to cast a double six when he needed it, becoming so arrogant that he would not accept me as his partner. "You are an E.P". he declared. "What pray is an E.P., Findlay" I demanded. "Useless fart, of course" he replied. I never mastered the art of spelling and never have to this day; but something seemed to be wrong. Such words were unheard and unwritten in the refined aura of the Canford classrooms! Perhaps they had kept Findlay so busy playing rugby, football and running up mountains at Sedbergh that there had been no time spelling. To tell the truth I never got to the bottom of it, but there was a war going on. Hitler seemed to be winning it, so I let the matter pass!

Montrose housed a busy flying training school, operating Airspeed Oxfords and Miles Masters. On the station we were tolerated with mixed emotions. Our aeroplanes were envied, but our airmen did not quite match up to the servile demeanour expected in a flying training school. Inevitably their flying programme would be interrupted by repeated operational scrambles with very lights fired from the watch office to warn training aircraft out of the way while we took off. Unfortunately some pupils were too slow. One of the Masters got in the way and clattered into my aircraft as we careered out from our dispersal. Fortunately there were no injuries – we faced a nerve-wracking enquiry as the result of which the Fighters and myself, as Section Leader in particular, were found one-third to blame; but I went unpunished and unrepentant. Indeed I was lucky to be alive because this Master was carrying a practice bomb which could easily have exploded and blown us all to kingdom come. Maybe another of my charmed lives had been used up.

Meanwhile Hitler was driving all before him in Norway. We became involved as the result of a phone message from Group at Newcastle to expect survivors from a Squadron of Blenheims which had been sowing mines in the Skagerrack; but had barely enough fuel to reach Scotland. Dunlop hurried off to the Station Headquarters where he requested a meeting with the Station Commander. He was told rather frostily that the Group Captain was engaged at a meeting with the Colonel of the Home Guard and could not see him. In consequence no orders could be given for the laying of a flare path. By this time glim lamps had been replaced by more practical equipment. Dunlop Urie, who normally maintained an unperturbable sang froid, returned to the dispersal disgusted and frustrated. Displaying considerable courage and initiative he then led a party of our stalwart auxiliary airmen to the night flying hanger. There they broke in and removed the night flying equipment and got a flare path laid in time to save a number of Blenheims with wounded men on board. They just managed to scrape across the coast of Scotland to land at Montrose with their tanks almost empty. Indeed, one Blenheim with a completely bald pilot affectionately referred to by his crew as "Curly" ran out of fuel on landing, and could not even taxi in. I think they were grateful. We certainly had some fun in the mess with Curly and his surviving pals from the Skagerrack. The Station, however, were after Dunlop's blood, whereas he should have been a given a medal. Fortunately 13 Group managed to smooth the ruffled Training Commands feathers.

I have pleasant memories of Montrose. The mess was comfortable and the beer, which was brewed locally by a Newcastle company, was the best I had ever tasted. Our cars ran well on a little extra 100 octane petrol milked from the bowser, without which we could have been stranded carless as the result of frequent moves which gobbled up petrol. The Montrose people were very hospitable.

The flying instructors, who included some RFC pilots in their forties, were men of steel charging off into the black with night flying pupils. They did a real job for the RAF and must have trained hundreds of pilots. Sergeant Cameron, later Marshal of the Royal Air Force, Lord Cameron of Balhousie. was one of the early pupils there at that time. He is said to have been so impressed by A Flight 602 that after training he applied for Fighters in which he later served with great distinction. Another future Marshal of the Royal Air Force, Squadron Leader John Grandy was Chief Instructor. He was itching to fly a Spitfire, so with some trepidation I lent him mine, which I am glad to say he returned to me in one piece.

At Montrose we got a new pilot from the RAF Reserve of Officers, Pilot Officer W H Coverley, who was inevitably nicknamed "Roger". The strict training command regime on the station did not appeal to Roger, nor did he appeal to them. He was anti-bullshit and the pomposity typified by his bete noir the Station Commander ("the Grouper"). Luckily he was beyond their reach so continued to regale us with his comments on the way things were done at RAF Montrose. He was dead keen, and made good progress in his flying. Roger was always accompanied by his bulldog "Spud", a ferocious looking creature with a beautiful sunny nature. Spud had one serious weakness. He was fascinated and devoted to noisy machines. For Spud the Spitfire was irresistible. Despite our efforts to restrain him he would jump up at the props. Finally he jumped once too often and fell wounded onto the tarmac. To our amazement all that had happened was that the propeller had nicked out one of his toes. Later on our return to Edinburgh Roger borrowed my Austin 8 for a visit to Edinburgh on his day off. Spud was in the back. As they were motoring along Princes Street a very loud motor bike passed in the other direction. Out leapt Spud and chased it all the way along to the far end. It took Roger, most of the day to collect him.

In May we oscillated between Montrose and Drem, where the hanger maintenance was done. During this period we saw little of our CO, George Pinkerton, who must have had his hands full with flights and sections moving around - all throwing up problems.

On the 11th May 1940 'A' flight moved to Dyce where we joined in with 603 for the first time. During our short stay George (known as "Sheep") Gilroy and I were ordered about 2.00 am to investigate a bogey at 25,000 feet. As I was climbing up through the night I decided on plenty of oxygen and gave myself an extra 5,000 foot dose. On the way up the R.T. was infested with music and German voices singing, but at 25,000 feet there was no enemy to be seen. Suddenly I began to feel happy and lightheaded. More oxygen perhaps? Then I saw it; the oxygen tube was hanging down lose and disconnected to my mask. There was no time to connect it because I had been without oxygen and was in the process of passing out, so down I went to 15,000 feet in double quick time. Woken from my slumbers and in a hurry to get off the ground I had omitted the elementary precaution of connecting my oxygen tube, and then my attention had been distracted by that wretched German singing. It was a strange business. I have never met anyone else who encountered a similar experience. I was probably hamming into a German programme transmitting from an unusual range as far as Aberdeen.

Soon after this incident, just before we returned to Montrose on the 16th May, I was leading Red Section off the Aberdeen coastline when Dyce control came on the air. The controller's voice announced in an unruffled and rather languid voice, "Red Leader are you receiving?" Answer - "Yes" "300 plus approaching you from the east". "Good God - curtains for Aberdeen". Apart from that we were going to be out numbered by one hundred to one. I called Control - "Message received. I have three aircraft. Can you send up reinforcements?" Answer came there are none! It was probably a flock of geese having fun with the radar. All the same I got the impression we might have been better served by Turnhouse control, under which we came once more on our return to Drem at the end of May.

CHAPTER 9
DREM AGAIN

As June began the Allies were in full retreat before the victorious German army, falling back on the port of Dunkirk. Our Fighter Squadrons were thrown in against heavy odds to cover the evacuation. The enemy bombers fighting over their own ground were able to reign destruction on the troops far below. They were heavily guarded by their fighters hovering above them at a great height. Against these forces our Squadrons just melted away. 602 were held in reserve at Drem until the 3rd June when we were sitting in our aircraft at standby for take off to an undisclosed destination. Our baggage was already loaded into a waiting converted airliner. The message to stand down came in the early afternoon. We were no longer required. The evacuation was completed on the 4th June by which time a quarter of Fighter Command were out of action with many of our best pilots dead. In 602 we had been saved by the bell. It was rather ignominious, but just as well because we were good and ready for what was to come in August and September.

605 County of Warwick Squadron, who had sustained heavy casualties, soon arrived at Drem with a handful of their remaining officers. Their Commanding Officer, Walter Churchill, was a real leader, full of initiative and enthusiasm. Without much warning both Squadrons were ordered on parade. The 602 pilots were looking indecently fit and healthy beside the 605 survivors. Douglas Farquhar suddenly appeared from his station at Martlesham Heath. Then came an aeroplane from which descended His Majesty George VI, accompanied by the Marshal of the RAF (Boom) Trenchard and Sir Louis Gregg. The King inspected the troops and pinned a medal on Walter.

605 soon began to build themselves up. Walter Churchill was not slow to spot Archie McKellar's potential and offered him a flight with 605 with promotion to Flight Lieutenant which he accepted. But if we lost one good man we got another in the shape of C J (Micky) Mount an Auxiliary from 600 Squadron who had been for many months flying Birdy Saul (as his personal assistant) around his group in a Percival Proctor. Micky was keen to join the fray so Birdy let us have him in exchange for Sprat, who was well suited to be his Personal Assistant. A Flight got Mount who took over the flight after I was wounded on 26th August. He survived the whole of the Battle of Britain, receiving the DFC in recognition of his efforts.

He was a mild and deceptively unwarlike figure blessed with the usual 602 sense of fun. He went on to command squadrons in the Western Desert and was eventually awarded the DSO and a permanent commission in the RAF, retiring as an Air Commodore.

About the same time we got Nigel Rose, a young pilot officer, who proved a real asset on the ground soon developing into a reliable fighter pilot. He recently showed me some of his letters to his parents at the time telling them how much he was enjoying 'A' Flight -

Fake game of chess - Drem 1940
Donald Jack, P J Strong, Archie McKellar, Cyril Babbage, Hector MacLean

which is good to know. Rose survived the Battle of Britain to which he made a useful contribution.

'B' Flight had acquired some able recruits including Pat Lyall, Sergeant Moody, and Sergeant Whipps. Lyall proved to a daring fighter pilot with incredible eyesight. It is said that his combat report would give the colour of the victimís hair. Perhaps he was rumoured just too good to last. Both he and Moody were soon commissioned Pilot Officers. The latter was so handsome that he was in

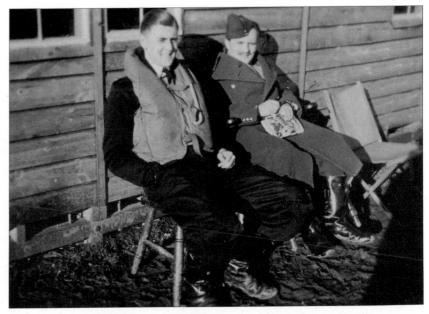

Sandy Johnstone and Archie McKellar at Drem
March 1940

demand at parties because he attracted girls like bees to a honey pot. Before disappearing for ever over the Channel in the Battle of Britain Pilot Officer Moody had made a spectacular parachute descent into the grounds of a girls' school where he was enthusiastically received.

Sadly Sergeant Elcombe and Sergeant Whipps who joined us about this time did not survive the war. Elcombe was reported missing in the Battle of Britain. Sergeant Whipps was killed later.

About this time Group Captain Charles Keary completed his tour of command at Drem and was to our delight succeeded by the legendary Wing Commander Richard ("Batchy") Atcherley of Schneider trophy fame. Things soon began to happen at Drem. The aircraft, which had been bunched in vulnerable little groups, were soon dispersed well apart in bomb blast enclaves built in a hollow E with substantial surrounding earth barriers. God knows why it had not been done before!

Batchy and his twin brother had been the perpetrators of endless "blacks" without getting the sack. The RAF must have appreciated real gold when they got it. He ruled with a light touch and quick reactions. Sandy got on well with him and tells of an airman who passed them on a path at Drem. "Fine day, Sir" said the man, an obvious admirer. "It's a salute I want from you young man" said Batchy, "not a weather report". Looking to the future Atcherley realised the potential to the RAF for schoolboys from establishments such as Fettes. To this end he organised parties of young Fettesians who came down to Drem to labour towards the war effort on the aerodrome. He rewarded them with hair raising trips in a Blenheim. Batchy messed with the pilots. One evening he asked me what I was doing. The cinema in North Berwick, I thought. "I will come with you," he said. So off we went - very democratic with no loss of authority.

Batchy soon got to grips with the night flying situation. The Germans had to be dealt with but in his own words "The main enemies were Isaac Newton and the Reaper". He was not prepared to have pilots and aircraft put at unnecessary risk by bad lighting while landing at night. He, therefore, evolved his own system to be known as "Drem lighting" which consisted of glim lamps situated in the fields outside the aerodrome just inside the circuit path of an aircraft approaching to land. These lamps were to be wired up to the watch office and switched on at the vital moments when needed. Sandy did the air test, and it worked. Drem lighting became quite famous.

About this time two important modifications were made to the Spitfire I. The De Havilland variable pitch propeller (fine for take off, and course for normal flying) was replaced like magic in all our aircraft within a matter of days by the new constant speed propeller (the ROTOL). By this device the pitch of the propeller would adjust automatically to suit any chosen throttle setting giving an overall improved engine performance. Then at last we got a sheet of steel armour plate fitted to the back of the pilot's seat. As the loser in an air combat usually finishes with a bullet in his back the Fighter Commandís refusal to our request for armour plate seems, in retrospect, about as perverse as their bullet grouping policy. The reason given was a possible reduction of three miles an hour in top speed due to the extra weight of the steel. I suppose the surviving Hurricane pilots from the Expeditionary Force, returning before Dunkirk, must have told them the facts of life. The loss of three miles an hour would be of no great interest to a dead pilot!

A further gift from on high had been a humble crow bar for each aircraft. In cases of emergency, such as a forced landing or encountering an unexpected obstruction such as a bomb crater, a single seater fighter could not only go on its nose, but could finish up on its back trapping the pilot in the cockpit under his perspex canopy. This did, I think, happen from time to time in Fighter Command who woke up to the possibility of their pilots being unable to bale out as the result of enemy attack causing a jam in the sliding perspex hood. In consequence our aircraft were in due course equipped with a small 18 inch crow bar neatly stored in the wall of the cockpit. This could be used in emergency to lever off the hood allowing the pilot to escape.

The crow bar fitted to my Spitfire, 'H' for Harry, on my last flight with the Squadron is on view in the 602 Museum. One might wonder how this artefact was acquired! It was, in fact, "whipped" by one of our airmen who must have thought the aircraft was due for the scrap heap. After the Third Reich had been successfully committed to the dustbin of history our man set himself up as a fishmonger, but over the years began to doubt his right to this particular souvenir from the Battle of Britain. Perhaps MacLean the pilot should have its custody. Then in the early eighties he received a surprise customer at his shop in Staines. It was none other than his war time Commanding Officer, now Air Vice-Marshal A V R Johnstone. After an enjoyable crack together about old times the crow bar was produced, and duly returned to me by Sandy Johnstone, and then presented to the Museum.

At the end of June 1940 George Pinkerton, after spells in command of 65 and 602 Squadrons, was posted to Sector Control, Turnhouse. He was succeeded as Commanding Officer of 602 by Flight Lieutenant A V R Johnstone of 'B' Flight. Soon after George was promoted Acting Wing Commander and received the command of a unique and rather splendid outfit based near the Port of Liverpool known as the Merchant Ship Fighter Unit (MSU). Their role was to provide the unfortunate merchant ships sailing in our Russian conveys with a Hawker Hurricane which cold be violently launched at sea by a special catapult apparatus installed forward of the bridge. The Hurricane would fly off and attack the enemy. Unfortunately there was no going back; so into the icy sea would go the Hurricane and its pilot who could scarcely survive the cold more than a minute before being picked up. George was uniquely qualified to command this bizarre operation. He not only excelled as a practical improviser in everything mechanical, but was also had a shrewd knack of dealing with difficulties as they arose. He made a success of the MSU until it was disbanded, after which he was awarded the OBE and promoted Acting Group Captain commanding a RAF station near Dundee. He completed his service as Group Captain Training at 12 Group Hucknall. George never lost his dour canny ways of dealing with many problems which came his way.

In 1945, on the very morning the atom bomb fell on Hiroshima, Sandy and I were on a

'First flight by night'
Hector MacLean in a Hawker Hind over Tait's Tower
at the Empire Exhibition, Bellahouston Park, Glasgow in October 1938.
Painting by Dugald Cameron

I

'Battle over the Forth'

Flt Lt George Pinkerton in Spitfire I L1019 'LO-S' attacking and downing a Ju88 of KG30
over the Firth of Forth near Crail on the afternoon of 16 October 1939.

Painting by Dugald Cameron

II

'Battle of Britain'
The Portsmouth raid in the early afternoon of 26 August 1940.
Painting by Anthony Saunders

III

Wapiti I, J9863
October 1933

Spitfire I, K9970 'ZT-D'
July 1939

Spitfire Ia, X4162 'LO-J'
September 1940

visit to Watnall, having breakfast in the mess. Sandy, still an Auxiliary Officer, was awaiting the result of his application for a regular commission in the RAF. We sat spell bound by the story reported in our newspapers. George put his paper down. "Well that's it Sandy, no more permanent commissions now - all they'll need is Portal (Chief of the Air Staff) and one aircraft"!

By mid June 1940, Batchy was still dis-satisfied with our dispersal. No doubt he anticipated heavy attacks when the enemy had drawn breath after Dunkirk. One flight was despatched each night to Macmerry, an airfield near Tranent which had accommodation for troops, and was occupied as a holding base for the army. 'A' Flight was warmly received by a detachment of the Royal Scots Greys. A splendid evening was spent in their mess. Unfortunately when it came to 'B' Flight's first visit matters had taken a very different turn. The Greys had been replaced by the 10th Royal Scots, a bunch of tough suspicious Edinburgh soldiers who had not been warned of the usual nocturnal invasion from Drem. On taxiing up to his dispersal point Findlay was forced out of his aeroplane at gun point and frog marched to the guard room to explain his presence. Taken by surprise the Guardians of Macmerry must have thought their last hour had come - a daring invasion by single seater fighters! Relations were a trifle strained while the 10th Royal Scots remained at Macmerry. In retrospect one can scarcely blame them for keeping up their guard until they found out what it was all about.

By this time we were becoming recognised voices in North Berwick and Gullane sitting rooms with their radios tuned into our operating frequency. However, we continued to enjoy local support and popularity despite the ribald language on the intercom to which they had been exposed.

It is certain there were spies in Edinburgh and North Berwick, and probably one much nearer home in Drem. On one occasion the spy must have over played his hand. Although I did not hear it there was a broadcast in which Lord Haw Haw announced from Germany that a number of 602 officers had been invited to a party that night to be given by a North Berwick hostess. It was, in fact, quite true.

An account of our time at Drem would be incomplete without reference to 609 (West Riding) Squadron of the Auxiliary Air Force which was just forming at Yeadon, near Leeds, when I dropped in there for lunch on the way to Tangmere in 1936. We got to know quite a number of their pilots including Pip Barron, Paul Edge, Beaumont, John Bisdee and John Dundas, elder brother of Hugh Dundas an auxiliary who became an outstanding fighter-bomber leader in the Italian campaign. John Dundas became a friend I was soon to lose. Squadron Leader Geoffrey Ambler, a popular but rather elderly Commanding Officer of 609, was in due course replaced by Horace Stanley Darley who had been briefly our Adjutant at Abbotsinch. The Squadron did brilliantly at Warmwell. Dundas shot down a German ace, Helmut Weiss near the Needles off the Isle of Wight, only to be destroyed himself by the German pilot's wing man.

By this time we had a new Adjutant, Flight Lieutenant "Crackers" Douglas a veteran of the Great War. Ding Dong and Andrew Rintoul had long since departed into the higher echelons of Administration and Accountancy. Crackers fitted in well but; as the name suggests, was one to crack a social whip. One evening after a few refreshments in the mess to gain flying speed he set off to sample the bright lights behind the black out curtains in Edinburgh. For this purpose he borrowed Donald Jack's motor car for the excursion. He returned the car next morning in working condition. On further inspection, however, Donald noticed some rather suspicious scratches on the roof. When questioned Crackers had to admit that there had been an incident. Indeed he had rolled the car right over and back again on to its wheels. He had then been able to continue his journey. He must have been one of the few who had achieved a slow roll in a motor car.

Just after the beginning of our first stay at Drem, Flight Lieutenant Cairns Smith and Flight Lieutenant Bill Scarnell, who held the Military Medal from the Great War, were posted to us as Operations Officers. Their duty it was to man the telephones at the dispersal, and maintain a continuous presence while the pilots came and went on readiness. As there were only two of them they must have been at it about 84 hours each per week; but they never complained. Our Ops officers made tea for the boys and put up with a good deal of cheeky banter. All Cairns got for his pains was to be known as "Mrs Cairns" which was a bit much for an RFC pilot from the Great War who had been an Honorary Instructor at the Scottish Flying Club. These qualifications proved of great value because Group and Sector Controllers were prepared to take their advice before sending us off at night in suicidal weather conditions. Cairns certainly saved my bacon on one such occasion. Bill Scarnell and Mrs Cairns were too good to last. They were much missed when they were posted away to another sphere of operations.

The Squadron had another pal at Station Headquarters who was a Lancastrian by name Flying Officer Fred Weildon DSO, a veteran from the Great War. He was Assistant Station Adjutant. He worked under the Squadron Leader administration known as "nippy Wardle".

Fred was, in a sense, our friend at court and never hesitated to express his views in forthright Lancastrian tones, particularly on the subject of station headquarters, including his Chief. "That Nippy cum four o'clock you can't see his ass for doost". With Nippy gone Fred would soon be in the mess himself for a glass of sherry - his favourite tipple. One evening after a few starters, and with a couple of bottles under his arm and another in hand, he set out for his house in North Berwick with an invitation for those present to pay him a call later on. Always keen on good works, and in order to save Fred from excessive damage to his liver, we decided to take him up on the invitation; so presented ourselves on his doorstep about 9.30 pm. We were greeted by a swaying but surprisingly sober figure shaking his head "Sorry boys, sherry's all dun".

Sherry was much favoured as a drink in Fighter Command. It never ceased to amaze me that, despite the shipping problems, the supply outlasted Hitler. Whisky, on the other hand, which was produced locally, was much harder to come by. There was always plenty of beer, and one could usually get gin or rum.

In the summer of 1940 RAF Station Drem, and 602 Squadron on the ground were well administered in an unobtrusive way by veterans such as Fred, Nippy and Crackers Douglas who did many of these dull tasks in the line of duty without much recognition.

On 10th June an East Coast haar descended on Drem. Then it began to lift which enabled Dunlop and myself, flying as red section, to get off to fly cover for an inbound convoy of ships. No sooner were we on our way than up again rose the haar. We were hastily recalled but the message came too late, and by the time we got back the whole aerodrome was covered to a depth of about twenty-five feet. Dunlop went in first and disappeared into the fog. As he needed time to get clear I hung around till I reckoned he must have made it. No report of a crash had come through on the RT. The haar was still rising. It was to be my first completely blind landing. After a trial approach in I went. I cannot remember if I actually saw the ground or just guessed. The Spitfire came to rest with a collapsed oleo leg. Happily it was soon repaired on the station.

After the war Dunlop and I, who became patners in our legal firm, once more nearly came to grief in the late fifties. At the end of the day we had stayed on in the strong room to clear out a host of papers, many of which had been retained since Edwardian times. Suddenly there was a shattering clang as our elderly despatch clerk, who was almost stone deaf, slammed shut the huge steel fire proof door. Horrors – by the next morning we could be asphyxiated. Urgently I seized an empty steel trust box and crashed it against the door making just enough noise to alert the old man before he went for his coat. Dunlop and I went down to the club for a large whisky. We must have been born survivors.

Towards the end of our spell at Drem, on 24th June 1940, the Squadron achieved a unique success. An enemy snooper decided to visit suicide alley on a fine moonlight night. The search lights got him returning over North Berwick. Fortunately the redoubtable Sergeant Andrew McDowall was on patrol and in position to latch on to his tail. We were then treated to a unforgettable sight – a red stream of fire from the fighter and the destruction of the target in full view from the ground. The enemy disappeared and, I think, crashed into the sea somewhere near Dunbar. It was a magnificent performance, but pure bad luck or bad judgement on the part of the enemy who could quite well have come and gone without going anywhere near the search lights on the south side of the Forth

After McDowall's victory the Squadron was still in luck. On 26th June Sandy Johnstone was on patrol at night between Dalkeith and Musselburgh. Following an alert from control at Turnhouse three search lights coned an aircraft. Sandy raced in behind expecting another friendly aircraft caught like a moth in the dazzling lights. To his surprise it was a Heinkel 111 with German markings bathed in light, squirming around to avoid its tormentors. Johnstone opened fire but was overtaking so fast that he only avoided collision by falling below out of control into the darkness under full power and with his instruments all over the place. With great skill Sandy rapidly sorted himself out and was up again behind the Heinkel which he despatched before it ran out of the searchlight cone. It was a fine exhibition of quick wits and skilful flying. On both occasions we were fortunate to have had above average pilots on patrol who were able to demonstrate what could be done in good conditions with the help of searchlights. These victories must have been a great boost for our searchlight crews who had been well and truly on their toes. Having said that our success did little to prove that day fighters could ever amount to an effective defence against the night raider. This became all too obvious when Hitler switched his attentions to London by night. Indeed, our success at Drem may partly explain why, at the height of the Battle of Britain when the Squadron had been heavily engaged all day, some of us were still ordered to do night readiness when we were thoroughly exhausted.

On the departure of George Pinkerton to the Control Room at Turnhouse on 4th July the command passed to Sandy Johnstone, Senior Flight Commander. George and Sandy were as different as two men could be. Both were highly competent pilots. George already in his thirties was dour, meticulous, deliberate and shrewd. Sandy in contrast is accurately described by the Duke of Hamilton in his foreword to "Where No Angels Dwell" in these words:- "For me this book recalls a particular day in 1934 when as Commanding Officer of 602 Squadron I had to interview an infectiously light-hearted, enthusiastic young man who was eager to join us. He was Sandy Johnstone who was to become one of the Squadronís most gallant members and successful war time leaders".

At this point in time, with the war going from bad to worse, Sandy's appointment was opportune. With his experience as an Instructor at Prestwick he was not only younger but had many more hours in his log book than the rest of us. He flew like an ace, but more importantly he had already demonstrated that he could shoot like an ace. Although Sandy must have had his worries they never showed. His light hearted approach was good for morale. These qualities were just what were needed when he led the Squadron to Westhampnett. Under his leadership 602 is believed to have destroyed about eighty enemy aircraft, and was the second highest scoring Squadron in Fighter Command. Despite the atom bomb and George Pinkertonís gloomy predictions there was still room in the RAF for Sandy who got his permanent commission after the war. He rose rapidly in the Service enjoying a succession of interesting appointments which are described in his books. Among these tasks he was largely responsible for launching the Malayan Airforce which led to his command of our air forces in the Borneo emergency. He was finally promoted to Air Vice Marshal and appointed a Commander of the Bath.

On 7th July Findlay Boyd, Roger and I destroyed a Ju88.

Meanwhile our presence at Drem was becoming uncomfortable. The enemy were obviously brewing up a major offensive. On the side lines in Scotland we felt like geese being fattened for Christmas. All the same we were good and ready with an experienced and enthusiastic Commanding Officer.

CHAPTER 10
THE BATTLE OF BRITAIN

On 13th August 1940 Sandy Johnstone led the Squadron from Drem to Westhampnett, which was a huge meadow on the Goodwood Estate about two miles east of Chichester.

The first phase of the battle had been a challenge by the German Air Force, and the beginning of a deliberate attempt to eliminate Fighter Command fought out over the British shipping in the English Channel. This phase was almost over, but to our surprise the enemy were still wheeling round Sussex engaged in an air battle as we thundered in strict radio silence across Goodwood Race Course, situated in the South Downs just north of our destination. On landing we were greeted by Group Captain Jack Boret, Station Commander at Tangmere our parent station. To my surprise he seemed disappointed we had not come in Hurricanes. He was worried because our new parent station had not been given any Spitfire spare parts.

The Hurricane, although slower than the Spitfire, was more effective against German bombers. Because of the way the wheels were retracted the eight machine guns were grouped closer together, making the Hurricane a better firing platform. The superior speed of the Spitfire made it a better bet for taking on the Messerschmitt 109 and the new Focke-Wulf 190 fighters. The controllers soon got the hang of this and, where possible, allotted us to deter the fighter escorts.

Causalities had been particularly heavy for 145 Squadron whom we were relieving at Westhampnett. After parking at our dispersal points we wandered across the road to the officers' mess in Woodcote Farmhouse. Paul Webb greeted A Flight at the door. "Come in" he said "and meet 145 - great chaps both of them". Indeed the great chaps turned out to be two rather disconsolate young officers sitting at the foot of the stairs clutching a few personal possessions waiting for their transport. In fact four pilots of 145 Squadron, including Johnny Peel their C.O., had survived. Peel, although shot through the arm, had managed to get his Hurricane down without its ailerons – quite a feat.

Fortunately we were to operate from this unknown satellite airfield, the advantage of which became clear on the 16th August when Tangmere was heavily bombed by Ju87

(Stuka) bombers reducing it to a domestic shambles, but with no effective damage to the grass airfield. The warning came too late. Nasty crumps from the direction of Tangmere. 602 scrambled off the ground helter skelter. The last of the 87s were still overhead. Findlay Boyd, who rarely missed a trick, had taken off right behind an enemy bomber. He destroyed it before he had even pumped his wheels up demonstrating his quick wits and deadly aim. It was a special treat for the airmen.

Visiting Tangmere shortly after this attack I was shocked by the state of the station buildings. For our earthly needs at Westhampnett we had come under the aegis of Squadron Leader Drudge, Officer in Charge of Administration at Tangmere. Looking around the station I thought poor Drudge must be having a hell of a time, and must have been named for the occasion!

For the enemy these attacks on our Fighter Stations made sense, but I do not think they

"At readiness" - Spitfire I 'LO-B' 602 Squadron 'A' Flight Dispersal at Westhampnett

ever knocked one out. Holes on the airfield could be quickly filled in. The attacks brought our airmen and airwomen into the war at first hand, and they responded magnificently.

Nearly every day began with a flap about 8.00 am "Patrol Worthing 15,000 feet"; and then sometimes when we were still on the way up the order would come to pancake. The usual doubts arose as to whether sector control had got themselves into a muddle. One bright suggestion was that 8.00 am was the time for the radar operator concerned to shave allowing his mirror to glint on the tube. The patrol would thus only last long enough for the man to get his beard off!

We did not have to fight every day. Much of the time we were sitting beside our Nissan hut waiting for the field telephone to ring for a scramble, which quite often resulted in a false alarm, and quick pancake for more fuel. This often happened before breakfast when I suspect the German snoopers would come to have a look. They did not waste time - my section never caught one.

On the 18th August the enemy launched a huge force of Ju87s, heavily escorted by fighters, to bomb Ford, an airfield on the Sussex coast. The Squadron arrived just in time. A long queue of dive bombers was already going down. We latched in behind them hoping for easy kills, but the 109s were soon upon us. I got away with it untouched but Dunlop's aircraft was badly damaged by cannon fire. It was a miracle he managed to land what was left of his Spitfire at Westhampnett. He was then removed to hospital with multiple shrapnel wounds. During the sixties one piece was detected by an eye specialist still lurking just behind, but luckily not touching one of his eyes where it remains to this day.

At Ford the Squadron claimed six Ju87s destroyed. Post war analysis of the engagement revealed six actually destroyed at that time when claims tended to be exaggerated. The combat reports reflect credit on our Intelligence Officer, Flight Lieutenant Grazebrook, a young barrister. Together with other squadrons engaged in attacking Ju87s we apparently achieved a tactical victory. Stuka losses had been heavy. Ford may have been the last straw because I do not think these dive bombers were used again for attacking our fighter bases. Hitler's knee jerk decision to concentrate on London rather than our airfields may, of course, have been the decisive tactical factor. The Ju87 was, to my mind, a brilliant aeroplane of great value to the enemy who used it in support of their ground forces where our fighter defence was weak or absent as, for example, what happened later in Tunisia.

At the hospital, on his arrival, Dunlop found himself in the next bed to Flight Lieutenant Nicholson, a pal of ours at Drem, where he had commanded a flight in 72 Squadron. Nick was later awarded the V.C. for pressing home an attack while his own aircraft was well and truly on fire. He was, of course, suffering from burns, but his main problem arose from his final encounter with a patriotic farmer armed with a shotgun. This loyal fellow had assumed that all those dangling from a parachute must be Nazis. He, therefore, let Nick have both barrels in his bottom but luckily decided not to finish him off after landing. The immediate medical problem was to get the wide spread of pellets out of the V.Cs backside.

With Dunlop in hospital I assumed the role of Flight Commander, still in the rank of Flying Officer, although I was to be promoted Flight Lieutenant on the 3rd September.

Our contact with Tangmere and the outside world depended on what the GPO called a "Don 8 Line" draped across intervening hedges. On the 19th, if I remember correctly, the telephone rang in A Flight Nissan hut. It was the distant voice of a Wing Commander at White Waltham Aircraft Supply Depot. Sandy was not available so he had to deal with me. "How are you for aircraft?" he asked. Summoning all my peasant cunning I replied "Very bad, Sir, I am looking through the window at the daylight coming through the holes in my late Flight Commander's Spitfire". "How many do you want then" asked the Wing Commander. I gulped with surprise. "Six" I replied, hoping to get two, and a load of flannel about aircraft shortage. "We'll have them there within the hour" he said. And so it was - fifty minutes later the Air Transport Auxiliary (ATA) were orbiting Westhampnett in six new Spitfires, all with fitted with undercarriages which you did not have to pump up by hand. We were fully in business again. I tell this story not only in honour of the unnamed Wing Commander, but also in recognition of the work and wonderful achievement of Lord Beaverbrook at the Ministry of Aircraft Production. At the close of the Battle of Britain Fighter Command had more serviceable fighters than at the beginning.

When the weather permitted the struggle became more intense. We soon got a taste of the new Messerschmitt 110. A beautiful but ferocious twin engine fighter which spat death from its four 20 millimetre cannons. One of our sergeant pilots encountered one of these monsters head on. His description of the encounter given to Sandy was "My finger was on the button, I was numb with fear, the enemy blew up and I flew through him". He was lucky.

As the result of experience gained in the Spanish Civil War the more senior German pilots probably had the advantage, but the German fighters were operating over enemy territory, so once down they were out. From the coast of West Sussex it is a long way across the Channel which cut down the operation time their fighters could spend over Britain.

As I discovered when my engine failed during an attack near May Island, the carburettor float in the Merlin engine could jam upwards when with engine stoppage if the stick was rammed forward into a sudden dive. With direct injection the German engines were immune from this problem. Fortunately I had rehearsed in my mind what to do if the enemy got on my tail. The solution was soon to be put to the test. After making an attack at about 15,000 feet on a formation of bombers to my horror I saw glinting lines of tracer bullets streaming past my port wing.. A glance in my mirror revealed a queue of the brutes lined up for the feast. I escaped by a quick roll to starboard in a spiral power dive hopefully keeping down the carburettor float by centrifugal force and hoping my wings were stronger than those of my pursuers. Down at 10,000 feet I sighed with relief. Then I went up to retrieve my honour, but there they were waiting for me. Then they suddenly melted away. No doubt they were running out of fuel. He who fights and runs away lives to fight another day!

Some days were relatively quiet, presumably when the Luftwaffe didn't like the weather or were getting their act together; but most were busy days when they would mount attacks in the morning and the afternoon involving us in several patrols a day. On one such afternoon I was faced with an awkward problem which led to a row with Findlay Boyd, now Flight Lieutenant and Senior Flight Commander.

By this time we had got the scrambling time from readiness down from five to two minutes, or even less, during which we had to run out to the aircraft, climb in, strap up, connect the pilotís helmet to the RT and to the oxygen tube and then start the engine. The starter battery trolley would then be unplugged and withdrawn. After that now sweating and puffing the leader would make sure that all the Squadron props were turning before signalling with his arm and opening his throttle.

On this afternoon "Delny" control at Tangmere ordered off the Squadron to patrol high up at a point somewhere near Southampton. All the 'A' Flight props had just begun to turn and I looked across to 'B' Flight who were due to lead in the take off. To my surprise there was no sign of life at the dispersal. I called Findlay on the RT but got no answer. Meanwhile my engine temperature was rising rapidly. With the wisdom of hindsight I should perhaps have shut down the 'A' Flight engines, but my worry was the possibility of arriving late with insufficient height to engage the enemy. We waited until the engine temperatures were approaching danger point and then took off and then stayed in the vacinity of Westhampnett until 'B' Flight were off the ground. The next question was whether to carry on at reduced speed and let 'B' Flight catch up, or whether to try and get them in front which was for me an unrehearsed manoeuvre with twelve aircraft. Whatever I did would eat into operational time and might result in a 'cockup'. So on we went and I led the Squadron into the attack. When we got back Findlay was furious - I had no right to lead the Squadron and he would brook no excuse. There was no point in disputing the matter, he was probably right, and he certainly would have made a better job of it.

At this time I was increasingly worried about my shooting and my failure to report anything better than apparent damage. My kills to date were only shared with other pilots. Perhaps head on attacks might produce better results so I decided to try it out. The opportunity soon presented itself. A formation of about twenty-five bombers had slipped past and was on its way towards the Midlands. Forging ahead I turned back on them, head on, dropping my speed to about 160 miles an hour to get a quick burst head on at the leading aircraft. All I got was a puff of smoke from one of his engines. The technique obviously needed further rehearsal.

I led the flight for the last time on August 26th 1940. The Squadron intercepted two large bomber formations of about fifty bombers over Portsmouth. I think I remember two formations, one of Heinkel 111s and the other Dornier 17s known as the Flying Pencils. They were heavily escorted by Messerschmitt 109s lurking up in the sun above. Details of this battle are annexed to this chapter. My own part in it ended in disaster.

Sandy was leading the Squadron in 'B' flight. We attacked by flights - so in went 'A' Flight as quickly as possible before the 109s woke up. I don't know whether we scored but, as usual, when I broke off there was not a friendly fighter in sight, just bombers turning to go home. It seemed a pity to let them off the hook. I did not see any 109s so rather stupidly I followed the bomber formations back over the Channel. I had just broken off my second head on attack on the leading formation but failed to notice a 109 in my mirror. An awful thudding began followed immediately by a fiendish pain above my right ankle. My right foot, still in its shoe, was hanging lose with the ankle minced up with my trouser leg. I would have to bail out. I released my safety straps and gazed down at the vast expanse of blue sea 16,000 feet below. It looked calm and deceptively inviting - at least more inviting than my cockpit. The pain was getting worse every moment. In haste to avoid being hanged on leaving the aircraft I threw my helmet with RT and oxygen connections over the side. I hesitated. Poor chance of survival in the sea if I reached it. But hold it - the engine was still running, I tried the throttle. By the Grace of God the engine responded. I must get back to live - a wooden leg would do! I was about thirty miles south of Selsey Bill. The blood was dripping. Would there be enough to get me back? I pulled off my tie but there was nothing with which I could secure a tourniquet. There was no point in wasting time and energy, so I put the nose down and raced for home at about four hundred miles and hour. I was getting very nearly at the end of my tether, hoping to slump down on the first field in my path; but every single field was heavily obstructed with poles in anticipation of an air borne invasion. In fact, this stood me in good stead because I had no option but to press on to Tangmere where I suspected the medical services might be more sophisticated than Westhampnett. The airfield ahead was obstructed with damaged and taxiing aircraft. Two feet would be needed for the rudder without which a Spitfire would be uncontrollable on the ground, (Shades of the horror I saw enacted at Grangemouth). There was nothing for it but to switch off the engine and land with the wheels up minus safety straps. I was lucky to manage it without more than a small bruise on my brow on impact. Dragging the remainder of my right foot I succeeded in crawling out on to the ground in order to avoid fire which so often finishes off a crashed aircraft. This fate had overtaken an unfortunate American pilot in 601 Squadron who had been unable to get out of his Hurricane before it burst into flames on the ground at Tangmere.

In due course the medical orderlies arrived in an ambulance. I was glad to get morphia. One of them fainted, but that may have been my bad language! I had indeed been lucky, my attacker, the Me109, had disappeared without finishing me off, perhaps he had exhausted his ammunition or may have been getting low on fuel. My Spitfire made Tangmere with one strand of wire remaining on the elevator cable, and minus its rudder which was hanging on one hinge - so I am told. It is encouraging to know that the aircraft was, in due course, repaired and went back into service. It was one of the new ones, 'H' for Harry, supplied by Lord Beaverbrook from White Waltham.

I went by ambulance to St Richardís Hospital, Chichester, where I lay for eternity before chloroform and the surgeon. The delay was, in fact, deliberate in case I died of shock. I felt like wringing their necks. I came to later; pain still excruciating - right foot gone despite stupid assurances given by the nurses that they could save it. The surgeon presented me with the 20 millimetre explosive shell head taken from the shards of my shin. It had come in from behind, under the armour plate which did not reach down far enough below the back of the pilot's seat.

I was at St Richard's under morphia until my stay came to a sudden end, when the threat of invasion resulted in the decision to evacuate the hospital. According to Sandy's diary this happened on 10th September. The night before Paul Webb had been brought in. He was lucky to be alive after the attentions of a German fighter which had damaged his aircraft in a curious way. It went out of control when the speed fell below 200 miles an hour. Paul was too low to bale out so flew on till he saw a nice soft looking wood. He then pulled back his throttle and careered into the trees. The aeroplane went upside down and deposited him on the ground - and so to St Richard's. The next morning we were called about 4.00 am and given some disgusting sandwiches consisting of scraps of fat left over from the kitchen. We lay in bed well into the morning when the patients were eventually loaded into ambulances and driven into Chichester station, arriving just before one oíclock. Our hospital blankets were removed, and after some delay were replaced by railway blankets for which we had to sign receipts before being loaded on board.

At long last the hospital train set off for its mysterious destination. It consisted of empty coaches with brackets on the walls on each side to take the stretchers. The staff were an unconvincing weird bunch of women. I doubt if they were real nurses. They certainly did not do any nursing except pour urine down onto the railway track through a hole in the floor. The facilities were crude but it is good to know that in Britain we had these arrangements set up for dealing with such emergencies.

Paul Webb was still in his uniform with his arm trussed up and a bandage around his head. "I'll never forget this as long as I live" he said.

As the train rolled into Warwick station a wail went up from the railway nurses when they beheld the team of beautifully turned out nursing auxiliaries waiting for us on the platform, where I soon found myself lying on a stretcher minus the railway blankets. I had been without morphia since the night before at St Richards and the effect had long since worn off. Paul in his uniform was quickly identified and whisked away to a special four-berth American ambulance where he complained loudly that I was missing. In desperation I grabbed one of the uniformed ladies by the ankle, to be told indignantly that they were looking for two flying officers. Finally I got the message through that flying officers could be found in pyjamas, and did not necessarily have to be in uniform. After this I was borne off to the waiting US ambulance, but they had just picked up and loaded a stretcher containing another incumbent. "Take him out" shouted Paul from inside "it's the wrong man"; but like a medieval fugitive from justice hanging at the horns of a church alter the "wrong man" seized hold of the bars of the ambulance structure and refused to move. At this point those in charge suddenly realised there was still a vacant berth into which I was

Sandy Johnstone
Commanding Officer

War artist Cuthbert Orde
was commissioned by the
Air Ministry to make
drawings of various pilots.
Some of 602's Battle of
Britain men are seen on
these two pages.

Dunlop Urie
OC 'A' Flight to 18 August

Hector MacLean
OC 'A' Flight
18 – 26 August

Donald Jack
'A' Flight

Andrew McDowall
'A' Flight

"Mickey" Mount
OC 'A' Flight from 26 August

"Ian" Ferguson
'B' Flight

Findlay Boyd
OC 'B' Flight

Glyn Ritchie
'B' Flight

Paul Webb
'B' Flight

loaded. In the fullness of time we reached the Warnford Hospital, Leamington. I was at the end of my tether and demanded morphia to be told by the Matron, with a solemn reproving shake of the head, that it was habit forming. At this point I blew up!

Almost 3,000 air crew qualified for the Battle of Britain clasp on the 1939/45 star which is the mark of a participant in the Battle. Fighter Command won because there were enough pilots and aeroplanes left to render an invasion impossible during 1940. It was certainly not won by aces in Spitfires and Hurricanes, but our success owed much to a small number of very gifted fighter pilots. 602 Squadron produced three. Archie McKellar, Findlay Boyd and Sergeant Andrew McDowall. It is appropriate to tell something about these men to whom our country owes so much.

During the war a perceptive journalist likened Archie McKellar to Robert Louis Stevenson's famous character, Alan Breck Stewart. He was not far off the mark. Archie was born with two broken legs. He was small at 5' 4", strongly built and quite good looking with black curly hair. He had an air of grace about him. Inside was a bigger man, ambitious with self confidence, tempered by a great sense of fun. He was irrepressible - a bit of a showman; but not bumptious. In the years before 3rd September 1939 Archie, like all the officers and airmen who joined the Squadron, knew that sooner or later we must face and defeat Hitler - how better for Archie than in the air which was to prove his element. He took to it like a duck to water.

I think McKellar was inclined to live for the moment. I remember the day after the war was declared he started to moan about the Squadron being in the wrong place. "Why can't they send us to the London area where the Huns will be coming in every hour?" "Good heavens Archie" I said, "the war has only just begun". He sadly shook his head and replied with a groan "It'll all be over by Christmas and we wont get a look in". He was no strategist!

Archie was essentially a man of action who grasped very quickly how many beans made five in any situation. After school he was trained as a plasterer in his father's business. There is a story of young McKellar on pay day. A huge truculent workman called the whole business in question, including Archie. McKellar weighed in, all five feet four, fists flying, and reduced the man to rubble.

The late '30s were unsettling times for our generation. Our daily tasks seemed almost piffling when compared with what seemed to be coming. As a practical chap, Archie probably gave his father satisfaction and high hopes for the future. Needless to say he was always down at Abbotsinch before the rest of us for his evening flying two nights a week.

Seldom did he miss his three weekends out of four at Abbotsinch.

There is no doubt that Archie was fairly pleased with himself, although he knew his limitations He tended to push himself forward, but I do not think the other offices resented it. Keenness and enthusiasm were infectious qualities which were appreciated, not only by the officers, but by the airmen in his flight. From the pilots' point of view he would be a good man to have on our side when the trouble started.

I cannot reveal much about Archie's background and early life, but I would liken it to creation and launching of an unique rocket of skill and daring. The rocket was to be fired in 1939 reaching its zenith in August and September 1940 when, as Commander of 605 Squadron, he was to prove one of the most outstanding and successful leaders in Fighter Command. His leadership in the air was even more vital than his nineteen victories. Fortunately for Britain all his early life, his ambition and guts, gave us the right man at the right time.

Archie was killed on November 1st 1940, the day after the Battle officially closed. For that reason he is not recorded in the Roll of Honour for the Battle which he did so much to win. On November 1st he was worn out. This story I heard of his last day. He was not due to fly that morning when one of his Flight Commanders struggled back from leave exhausted by wartime train journeys. Archie said "Don't worry old boy have your breakfast, I'll do your readiness". He was gallant to the last - in the air and on the ground. He never collected his DSO or the bar to his DFC.

Archie knew well that he was unlikely to survive the Second World War; but that did not deter him. Looking back after all the years he recalls for me the poem read to us by the governess in the bottom form of my prep school which I think goes:-

> Up spake brave Horatious the keeper of the gate
> To every man upon this earth death commeth soon or late
> And how can man die better than facing fearful odds
> For the ashes of his fathers and the temples of his gods.

Robert Findlay Boyd, DSO, DFC and Bar was cast in a different mould. Educated in the spartan climate of mountain runs and rugby at Sedbergh, like Archie, he proved no scholar; but when it came to the things he liked and understood he rarely missed a trick. He had a passion for guns of all shapes and sizes.

As a pilot Findlay lacked Archie's panache; but I don't think he regarded that as important. Like Baron Richthofen and Mick Mannock, the two aces of the Great War who ran up the highest score of victories for their respective sides, Findlay regarded a fighter aeroplane as a gun platform. He was consumed with contempt and loathing for all Germans. This hatred was fuelled by the conduct of the Luftwaffe after their atrocities in Poland when they dive bombed and machine gunned refugees crowded on the Belgian roads.

In the air Findlay tended to wait for his opportunity. Then he would move in with rapid and devastating effect. He flew right through the war with very few breaks - Flight Commander, Squadron Commander, Wing Leader, and then as Acting Group Captain Operations in Burmah. Even when resting as a Station Commander at Eglinton in Northern Ireland he set off in a Spitfire flying low over the western Atlantic approaches beyond the Mull of Galloway. Sure enough there was a juicy four engined Condor snooping around our convoys. I doubt if they knew what hit them. There is no doubt the war took more out of Findlay than he had to give. He was never quite the same afterwards. He is said to have destroyed 28 enemy aircraft.

Wing Commander Andrew McDowall, RAFVR, DFM and Bar, was trained before the war at Prestwick. On the outbreak of war he was posted to 602 Squadron as a Sergeant Pilot. Early in 1940 he distinguished himself by destroying an enemy aircraft caught in the search lights over North Berwick, thereby proving that it really could just be done. Those of us on the ground had a ring side seat. First the illuminated target, then the stream of red tracer going straight in - an object lesson in cool accurate flying and good shooting. McDowall went on to become one of the top scoring pilots in Fighter Command. After receiving his commission he rose rapidly in the service. He destroyed 12 German aircraft.

There is a good story of his early days in the Squadron. As a Sergeant Pilot he was finding his pay somewhat inadequate compared with his peacetime emoluments from Mavor and Coulson in Bridgeton. With this in mind he approached Marcus Robinson, his Flight Commander. "The men putting up the huts behind the dispersal are getting £10 per week, we're only getting ten shilling a day. What can you do about it, Sir"? "Not much I'm afraid McDowall" answered Marcus Robinson. "But tell me this, which would you prefer, putting up the huts or flying Spitfires?" "Spitfires" answered McDowall. "Well there's your answer" replied his wily Flight Commander.

When Sergeant (Ginger) Whall came to us at Drem on 5th July 1940 his DFM was in the pipeline as a result of his service operating in Gladiators with 263 Squadron from a frozen lake in Norway. His destruction of three enemy aircraft as a Gladiator pilot was no mean achievement. It would appear from his entry in Kenneth Wynn's book that before his mysterious fatal crash landing at Lullington Whall had been involved in the destruction of about seven more enemy aircraft in the Battle of Britain. Taken together with his remarkable achievements in Norway Whall was clearly a star turn in the making and a great loss to the Squadron. Donald Jack who led Whall on his last patrol describes him as a shy retiring young man with corn coloured hair and pale eyelashes, almost an albino - with freckles. In the air he was aggressive and pressed home his attacks with dogged determination. Sandy Johnstone recalls him as being one of the best NCO pilots in 602, and only became aware of his previous record in Norway when his DFM came up. It was then realised what a gem we had flying with us. Sandy would have recommended Whall for a commission in due course, but he was left with little time during the battle to keep abreast of such administrative matters.

Paul Webb remembers Whall fashioning a small brass replica of a Spitfire. "Not a lot to say, but smiled readily which was good stuff in the rather tense atmosphere we lived in. He would have gone far if he had survived. One needed a big slice of luck you know."

After the 50th anniversary of the Battle much has been heard about Spitfires and Hurricanes; or more accurately too much about Spitfires and not enough about Hurricanes which outnumbered them by about two to one; and certainly not enough about our faithful airmen who served out the war in all their vital trades - undecorated and unsung.

The following account of the fourth raid against Portsmouth on 26th August 1940, which was my last operation, could be a way of illustrating one of these air battles fought in 1940. It begins with Sandy Johnstone's account as follows:-

"We were brought to readiness in the middle of lunch and scrambled to intercept a mixed bag of Heinkel 111s and Dornier 17s approaching Portsmouth from the south.

"The Controller did a first class job and positioned us 1,000 feet above the target with the sun behind us allowing us to spot the raiders from a long way off. The supporting Messerschmitts were out of sight although a sizeable force was to turn up soon after. Then something strange happened. I was about to give a ticking off to our chaps for misusing the RT when I suddenly realised I was listening to German voices. It appeared we were both using the same frequency and, although having no knowledge of the language it sounded from the flow of conversation that they were unaware of our presence. As soon as we dived towards the leading formation, however, we were assailed immediately by loud shouts of "achtung Schpitfeueren"! as our bullets began to take their toll. In spite of having taken Jerry by surprise the 11 Group bag was only six, others claimed as damaged before the remainder dived for cloud cover and turned for home.

"The escorting fighters were amongst us when two of our fellows were badly shot up. Hector MacLean stopped a cannon cell in his cockpit blowing off his foot. In spite of his grave injuries he managed to fly the Spitfire back to Tangmere to land with the wheels retracted.

"Cyril Babbage's aircraft was also badly damaged in the action forcing him to abandon it and take to his parachute. He was ultimately picked up by a rescue launch and put ashore at Bognor having suffered only minor injuries. I accounted for one Heinkel 111 in the action."

I have noted my own account of this raid as follows:-

We intercepted a large formation of Heinkels followed by another big formation of Do17s. 602 attacked the Heinkels after which the battle seemed to disintegrate. I then observed, with disappointment, the Dornier formation still apparently intact and returning towards France. I followed them and was severely wounded about thirty miles south of Selsey Bill after a head on attack on their leader, and fortunately I was able to reach Tangmere with my wheels up about ten minutes later.

For a raid of 50 bombers to cause so little damage it would appear they were badly disorganised by the defences.

Against a total force of 157 enemy aircraft 11 Group fielded 32 fighters and were lucky to lose no more than three pilots killed and five aircraft, including mine which was recovered. Two enemy fighters and five bombers were destroyed.

The main purpose of these large escorted bombing raids was to prepare for the invasion of Britain by the elimination of Fighter Command. On balance Portsmouth on 26th August must be ranked as a Luftwaffe failure in the overall context of the Battle of Britain.

CHAPTER 11
LORD DOWDING

Air Chief Marshal Lord Dowding of Bentley Priory was born at St Ninians Preparatory School, Moffat, where his father was the headmaster. Both father and son were educated at Winchester where Dowding joined the army class to avoid learning Greek verbs.

At the tender age of eight and a half I myself was sent to St Ninians which was still conducted in the Winchester tradition including the wearing of ghastly Eton collars which would not fit in between my shoulders and my chin. On the mantelpiece in the dining room was inscribed the famous motto "Manners Maketh Man". It is still there for the benefit of the ex RAF chaps who inhabit the place. I was never wholly convinced. There must I thought be a bit more to it than that! So it was with Dowding - not only good manners but also a will of steel which was needed to have Fighter Command prepared for the inevitable struggle against overwhelming odds.

After Winchester he went to Woolwich but did not score sufficient marks for the Royal Engineers so had to settle for the Gunners.

In 1914 at the age of 32, against his father's wishes, and at his own expense, he learnt to fly and went solo in an hour and forty minutes. He was in due course seconded from the Gunners and accepted into the RFC. He was sent to France as a Squadron Commander in 1915 and served there with distinction and later as a Staff Officer.

When the war was over many senior officers of the Royal Flying Corps, including Acting Brigadier

*Air Chief Marshal
Hugh Caswall Tremenheere Dowding*

117

General Dowding and Acting Brigadier General A C H MacLean, became surplus to establishment in the small new peacetime Royal Air Force. Both these officers, and many others, were reduced in rank and returned to their regiments in the Army, Campbell MacLean finding himself once more as an infantry Major in the Royal Scots. Fortunately for Britain General (Boom) Trenchard, the Chief of Air Staff, was persuaded by those who had worked with Dowding that a serious mistake had been made. He was thereafter recalled to the RAF in the rank of Group Captain.

Those who worked with "Stuffy" during the twenties and the thirties and during the earlier part of the Second World War are mostly dead and gone. What was he really like to work with? One can only guess. His nickname "Stuffy" gives us a clue. General Sir Frederick Pile, Commander in Chief of Anti-Aircraft Command whose guns came under Dowding's operational control, describes him as "a difficult man", "a self opinionated man", "a most determined man" and "a man who knew more than anybody else about all aspects of aerial warfare". He probably got it in a nutshell.

As a means of building up fighter morale, Field Commanders such as Montgomery made themselves known and impressed their personalities on those serving under their commands. Dowding never bothered with any of that. He wasn't interested in propaganda. He wasn't interested in publicity. He didn't have to bother because his Squadrons were well equipped and manned by enthusiasts from the humblest airmen to his Squadron and Station Commanders. The morale was there so there was no need to build up his own image. In contrast to the political bombast of Reichmarshal Goering, Chief of the German Luftwaffe, Dowding kept a low profile. Apart from Squadron Commanders, who were occasionally summoned to the presence, none of us in Scotland knew, or even saw, the Commander in Chief. At the time it seemed to us that his proper place was at his desk or, as one supposed, down the "hole" (as it was called) in the Command Operations Room - about 60 feet below the ground at Bentley Priory. That is where he went when things began to happen.

Despite this unassuming profile Dowding's pilots probably saved our country from attempted of invasion. If he had failed, or if the squadrons had failed, we might never have heard the names of brilliant commanders such as Montgomery, Alexander and Slim. They might never of had their chance.

Do not suppose for a moment that Dowding was indifferent to his squadrons or their morale. Indeed his son was serving as a pilot in one of them which must have added to his worries. The Commander in Chief knew that delegation was the key to success in war; as it is in business. His choice of Group Commanders was brilliant; particularly Air Vice Marshal Keith Park, Officer commanding 11 Group who was responsible for the defence of London and the south-east coast. We did not see much of the C-in-C, but we saw enough of our AOCs - sometimes a bit too much for comfort!

After the great naval Battle of Jutland there were some who criticised Lord Jellicoe, the Commander in Chief of the Grand Fleet, for over caution. In his defence it was pointed out that, although the Grand Fleet could never, by itself, have won the Great War, Jellicoe was the only man in Britain who could have lost it in the course of an afternoon. In Dowding's case there were no less than three occasions when he could have lost the Second World War.

First came his unique contribution in the pre-war years when our defences had been run down as the result of disarming politicians and others who should have known better; but preferred to bury their heads in the sand. It must have called for real determination by Dowding and others in the face of such political indifference to bring our air forces to a state of readiness by September 1939. Before his appointment to Fighter Command "Stuffy" was, I understand, the Air Ministry Staff Officer largely responsible for instigating these preparations.

From 1936 onwards the Volunteer Reserve took shape and grew rapidly at Prestwick and elsewhere. Together with the Empire Training Scheme and the VR the RAF was at last getting down to business.

The gathering storm in Europe and its implications for Great Britain were clear enough for those of us who would in the end be called upon to stop Hitler. It was equally clear that our preparations would never catch up with Germany, particularly in the air where we would be heavily outnumbered.

By a strange paradox it was during these dark days that our success was born out of our weakness. Under Dowding and his staff at Fighter Command a novel and unique weapon was forged - something the enemy had never bothered about; and didn't really bother about until it was too late. I have already made reference to the control and reporting system which was in operation by early 1939. Under Dowding grew not only the Fighter strength, but also the Observer Corps, the Coastal Radar Chain, the Raid Reporting System, the Filter Rooms and the Fighter Control Operations Rooms. By mid 1939 our fighters could be conserved on the ground until the last minute and then directed by R.T. straight to their quarry. By then the RT was functioning on HF (High Frequency). HF was soon replaced by VHF (Very High Frequency) with four channels which made all the difference in performance and adaptability. When war was declared the control and reporting system was working for large raids. Without it we could not have fought the Battle of Britain which would have been lost and the invasion launched with consequences about which we can only speculate.

Without Dowding's control and reporting organisation standing patrols would soon have exhausted all our engine hours leaving what was left on the ground to be destroyed from the air by bombs and machine gun fire.

There are two kinds of courage. Physical courage in the face of the enemy and moral courage - so often needed, not only when dealing with one's foes, but also with one's friends.

In the spring and early summer of 1940 we in Britain watched with horror the disintegration of the French Army and the evacuation of our best troops through Dunkirk leaving behind them almost all our whole stock of modern weapons.

Dunkirk posed a problem for RAF morale. Fighter Command had lost about a quarter of its pilots covering the evacuation, including some of the most experienced ones. They had done what they could against the Luftwaffe, who were attacking the beaches from high up in the sky operating from occupied airfields and out of sight of the unfortunate troops on the beaches who never saw our fighters and thought the air forces were doing nothing. After the evacuation RAF personnel in London were abused and even attacked.

Steps were taken by Winston Churchill who made some of his stirring speeches to the nation. 605 (County of Warwick) Squadron with a handful of remaining pilots were posted to Drem to recover and reform. Then out of the blue we were visited by His Majesty accompanied by Lord Trenchard and Sir Louis Gregg It was just what the boys needed.

During this period the Commander in Chief came under great and foolish pressure to save the already beaten French forces from collapse by throwing in Squadrons from Fighter Command. Fortunately for us all he refused and stood firm, loyally backed by Sir Cyril Newell, Chief of the Air Staff. His career was at stake but he did not waiver. His fighter strength was, in his opinion, already below what he reckoned was required to repel an invasion. Fortunately there were just enough of us left when the battle began in July. Once more the war could have been lost - this time over a desk.

After the Battle of Britain Dowding came in for his share of adverse criticism which is always easier with the benefit of hindsight. Seen from my level, far below, he was strong on strategy but not always sound on tactics. How else can one explain his continued acceptance of the initial bullet grouping, and his failure to alter it despite the protests of his pilots which must have been received from the Squadrons, including ourselves, and which were soon proved well founded by the prodigious expenditure of ammunition with so little result at the Battle of the Forth. One gets the impression that he was too stubborn too reverse the advice given by his staff in the face of growing evidence that they had got it wrong.

Fighter Command's initial refusal to contemplate armour plate behind the pilot's seat was, in my view, a fundamental tactical error which should have been obvious to any fighter pilot with RFC experience in the Great War. The whole object, to put it crudely, was to shoot your opponent "up the bum". The argument against armour plate was that the extra weight might reduce the maximum speed of the fighter by two or three miles per hour. To our way of thinking this was irrelevant if you happened to be dead before you opened your throttle. The loser in an air combat in the Great War and in the Second World War was almost always put out of action by enemy fire from astern, and it is certain that many of our pilots, who had to jump with their parachutes or who came back with an aeroplane riddled with bullets, would have died in their seats without armour plate. Fortunately it was fitted just in time. The outcome of the Battle of Britain depended on the survival of pilots even more than victories in combat. Without that armour plate who knows what could have happened. The whole course of the war might have been different.

Without the overall picture of the factors involved on 3rd September 1939 one should perhaps hesitate to condemn Fighter Command for their handling of the night flying problem which was fundamentally insoluble. The Blenheim was designed as a day bomber with a speed no greater than the German bombers which they could not catch even if they found one. Command, therefore, had no fully operational night fighters as such; and certainly nothing which could, by itself, be effective at night without ground and airborne radar. It was, I think, assumed with some justification, that the British public wanted to hear that our fighters had gone up. Command must have known that the public did not understand, and could not be expected to understand, that without search lights and without airborne radar, which was still in a crude undeveloped state, that there was no way of finding and destroying the enemy without far more search lights and radar, save by chance in moonlight conditions of clear visibility.

Those in command of the RAF at the beginning of the Second World War were all RFC pilots, some of whom had, in their own youth, been involved in hazardous and skilful night patrolling. I remember Wing Commander Otway Norwood, Senior Personnel Staff Officer at our Headquarters in Northern Ireland, an RFC pilot, telling me that he had done two hundred hours night flying over London searching, without success, for Zeppelins. His blind flying instruments consisted of two spirit levels, one bubble to keep the aircraft flying level and the other to maintain lateral trim. Even so he never got a Zep which, by all accounts, needed successful search light illumination. With feats like that in mind the older generation, no doubt, concluded we could do the same in Spitfires and Hurricanes; although, in the end with practice and experience, some pilots (to their credit) did achieve a modicum of success by night.

It may have come as a surprise for Dowding and his air staff when the war began that the Commanding Officers of crack regular units, such as 111 and 72, declined to have their Squadrons listed as night operational. Command wisely took no steps to force the issue. At that point, in my view from the bottom of the heap, Command were ill advised to accept without further enquiry an offer from a bunch of Scottish amateurs with very limited night flying experience to do what experienced regulars had declined to do. If they had faced the situation a number of lives would have been saved and a number of accidents avoided. In our case the life of a keen young sergeant pilot would not have been lost. Brydon's death and the near fatal excursion to Barrhead reservoir by Sandy Johnstone, a pilot with a thousand hours in his log book, should have been sufficient warning for Group and Command - also proof that the Regular COs had been right. In retrospect it might have been wiser to have concentrated more on night flying training and to devote more attention and energy to improving anti-aircraft shooting, something which the Germans were to do with horrible accuracy as our bombing offensive developed over Germany. I doubt if Britain would have been any worse off if the whole business had been delegated to anti-aircraft Command and the balloons; but it so easy to be wise after the event pontificating from an armchair sixty years later! I doubt if the Commander in Chief ever contemplated such a solution which would have produced a political storm, and would have been deeply resented by the people in London, which was the obvious target for an initial air attack. Following the declaration of war many of us anticipated an immediate air attack on London. Command had to be ready for it, but Hitler decided to keep us waiting. After doing their dirty work in Poland the Luftwaffe, who had been organised and trained for the support of the Germany army, were held back and made ready for the offensive operations which the Fuhrer had planned.

Anti-Aircraft Command were equipped with quick firing Bofers guns, effective up to 3,000 feet, firing on open sites. Above that was the realm of the 3.7" anti-aircraft gun which could reach a height of thirty thousand feet. Without radar, which came later, its gunners had to rely for height finding and target projection on relatively primitive equipment which became increasingly inaccurate the greater height at which the target arrived. More search lights were the key to the business, but with three Blenheim squadrons who could not catch the enemy and with untried and unproven anti-aircraft defences, the Commander-in-Chief had little choice; so he used the lot including his unsuitable day fighters.

The bullet grouping and armour plate were mistakes, but they were put right before the real trouble started. Night interception was a difficult problem and so remained until the development of Ground Control by GCI radar, and by guidance of AI (air interception) from within the night fighter itself. As the war developed these new developments began to pay off, but we never seemed to nibble down more than a few German bombers; whereas the German anti Aircraft defences became increasingly formidable.

Dowding's strategy and his magnificent achievement was to prevent the launching of a cross channel invasion which could not have succeeded unless the German bombers were left free from interference while neutralising our defences, including the Royal Navy, nor until their fighters could protect their barges and airborne landings from attacks by the RAF. For these and other reasons an invasion could scarcely succeed while Fighter Command remained an effective operational force. Fighter squadrons once committed to continuous battle tend to melt away. To keep his command in business Stuffy was right to drive 10 Group and 11 Group to the limit and keep the 12 Group and 13 Group squadrons as his uncommitted reserve. They were, as Napoleon would have said his "Mass de manoeuvre", or looked at in a different way - his last reserve, which indeed became very significant in the final stages of the Battle.

Much has been written about the big wing controversy which broke out after the Battle of Britain; but it has to be reviewed against the strategic scene for which the Commander in Chief was responsible.

Air Vice Marshal Trafford Lee Mallory at 12 Group was a rising star in the high command of the RAF. Although Fighter Command made considerable use of his squadrons to reinforce Air Vice Marshal Park's hard pressed squadrons in 11 Group, one can understand Lee Mallory's impatience, and the frustration of Squadron Leader Douglas Bader his Wing Leader at Duxford at being held back in reserve when they were convinced that large wings of fighters could achieve decisive results. The 12 Group Squadrons were, in fact, quite rightly deployed in large wings for the daylight defence of London at the perfect tactical moment. Their appearance in force must have come as an ugly surprise for the enemy approaching London who had, no doubt, been told that the RAF were on their last legs. 12 Group were, in my view, unleashed in the defence of London at exactly the right moment when the greater distance to London had cut the combat time available to the Me109 to about ten minutes.

12 Group were, in fact, geographically better placed for the operation of wings which take time to assemble, an operation which had not, at that time, been rehearsed. Indeed, this process could, I believe, be watched by our radar as the enemy were doing it over France, while our fighters sat conserving their fuel waiting for the raids to develop. When the moment came to scramble their fighters the 12 Group Squadrons had sufficient time to form up their wings. By contrast the 11 Group Squadrons, based south of London and near the coast, such as 602, would not have had enough time to form up with other squadrons in order to intercept the bombers before they could reach their targets. Unlike 12 Group, whose squadrons were wisely held in reserve, 11 Group had to deploy their dwindling force of experienced pilots to meet attacks developing simultaneously in different parts of the Group area. The deployment of individual flights and squadrons against heavy odds was proving surprisingly successful. The accepted doctrine in military circles is to exploit success. To have changed their tactics by deploying wings with the limited number of squadrons available, 11 Group could have made a bad mistake with serious consequences.

From what I have read in books by those who have written in detail about the battle, there is little evidence that in defence wing formations were any more effective than attacks by individual squadrons or flights. Later in the war wings were, initially under Lee Mallory's command, successfully employed in offensive fighter sweeps over enemy occupied territory, during which squadrons or flights could be detached by the Wing Leader as circumstances and opportunities arose; but I cannot believe that a formation of thirty-six or more aircraft could ever have been sufficiently manoeuvrable in defence against bombers. In my own limited experience the German fighters would arrive in wing strength above their bombers, some of which we were able to attack before the Me109s could get down to join the party. I saw it happen more than once.

On the subject of deploying of big wings I am reasonably sure that Dowding will be awarded the verdict by history.

In paying these tributes to the Commander in Chief and the officers and airmen under his command one tends to give the impression that Fighter Command won the war -which is nonsense. They did prevent the possibility of an invasion just as the Royal Navy and Coastal Command saved us from going down to starvation and defeat if the German submarines had won the Battle of the Atlantic.

Whether our remaining forces, disorganised and without their modern equipment left behind at Dunkirk could have held the invasion in the face of daylight bombing and overwhelming air cover is something we will never know. Fortunately we do not need to know!

The German invasion of Russia was launched five weeks late, on June 22nd 1941. Before the end of the year the German armies ground to a halt in the mud and snow without reaching Moscow and Leningrad. Those vital five weeks were needed for the invasion of the Balkans and Greece in order to prevent a British led allied flank attack from the south. With Britain under German occupation the Balkans and North Africa could have waited. Hitler could have attacked Russia at his convenience and there would have been no Alamein, no invasion of Italy and no Jews left in Europe. Things would have been very different in the Far East.

Since the Norman Conquest three men have tried to invade these islands - Philip of Spain, Napoleon and Hitler. On the third occasion, command in the first great air battle in history fell upon Hugh Dowding's shoulders. How different the role of the Commander-in-Chief on this occasion. Not for him the splendour of the quarter deck with the guns blazing. In contrast three months of knife edge anxiety - at his desk - on his telephones, his officers coming and going in the deep hole at Bentley Priory stuffed with telephones; and a plotting table manned by faithful airmen and airwomen - decisions in quick succession.

It was indeed different from the Spanish Armada and the Battle of Trafalgar - the panache and daring of Drake and Nelson were scarcely appropriate. In command was a terse reserved man of great professional ability, respected for his record, and trusted by those serving under him.

And so the end result was just the same as on the two previous occasions. Not a single enemy soldier set foot on these islands except on his way to a prison camp.

Once more, therefore, let us give thanks for the third time in our history for the right man, at the right time, in the right place.

CHAPTER 12
CONTROLLING

I spent the autumn of 1940 recuperating in Kilmacolm during which time the Luftwaffe was concentrating on London.

I was, however, getting restless in Kilmacolm. The war had only really begun and I was determined to see it through. It is curious that the possibility of defeat never seriously crossed my mind, but quite a number of people were, at that time, beginning to express their doubts. True we had saved ourselves from invasion, but to win the war rather a different matter. Meantime nothing seemed to be going right.

As operational flying was for the time being out of the question fighter control seemed the best way of utilising my experience.

In a previous chapter I have given a brief account of the control and reporting system as experienced by the pilot. It may now be of interest to bring the reader down to earth where most pilots finish by flying a desk!

During the autumn of 1940, although the stump of my right leg was still not completely healed it was possible to begin the fitting of an artificial limb. I, therefore, reported to Turnhouse and took delivery of it just before the New Year of 1941. To begin with the leg fitted well; so off we went into Edinburgh to celebrate the event. The next day I began a watching brief in the sector operations room at Turnhouse which was at that stage responsible for the defence against air attack for the whole of Scotland, with 602 and 141 at Prestwick, and 603 at Drem. In addition we had guns, search lights and balloons in the Clyde and Forth areas with a duty Antiaircraft Liaison Officer sitting beside the Controller. The important naval base at Rosyth was on our doorstep, so the Royal Navy was represented by an NLO (Naval Liaison Officer). This position was manned by a staff officer known as "Sailor Murray". I do not think there were any other NLOs so presumably he was on duty twenty-four hours a day and one hundred and sixty-eight hours a week. A story was current about the sailor who became bored with the proceedings during the wee small hours. Seizing his phone he asked for Group and demanded to be put through to Command and then, via Command and a series of naval establishments. Finally after going right round Britain he demanded the NLO Turnhouse. When the phone rang he was able to conduct a brief conversation with himself. I thought the GPO did him rather well!

Having spent about a fortnight watching the proceedings in the Sector Operations Room I was attached to Wing Commander ("Windy Joe") Bradford's controllers course at Woodlands, Clamphill near Stanmore in North London.

On my way to Stanmore I made friends on the train with a young officer from Newfoundland. He was keen to sample the delights of London town, and planned to spend that very evening in the Café de Paris which was all the rage at that time. He would be new to the London scene so would I go with him? I was tempted, but I was having leg fitting problems together with jagging pains, known as "pings", from the severed nerves in my stump. My fiancée, Marcia Dods, was in Scotland so would be unable to share our night out "on the tiles". Instead I went to bed early in the Strand Palace Hotel observing with satisfaction that I was only half way up the building. Sure enough the raid began but I was too lazy to go down to the shelter. With any luck a bomb with my name on it might not reach down to my level before exploding! I slept soundly at the Strand Palace but in the morning there was terrible news. The Café de Paris had been destroyed by a bomb which came through the roof and went straight through the dance floor. It was said that the guests were found – all killed by the blast still sitting at their tables. I thought sadly of my young Canadian friend. What a way to start a war – a lucky escape for me!

An appreciation of the Control and Reporting system at this late date enjoys the benefit of hindsight. When the war began most of the difficulties and problems already described had scarcely been revealed in practise. Many of the duty sector controllers were re-employed Reserve and Volunteer officers from the Great War who had to learn it all from scratch. Fortunately the war in the air over Britain did not really take off until the German offensive began in the spring of 1940, which gave Fighter Command many valuable months to sort out their Ops Room teething troubles, and to bring their Sector Controllers up to scratch. The young Squadron pilots naturally expected perfection but, of course, we never got it. Failures and cock-ups were a frequent subject of conversation. One story current at Drem concerned a large scale dummy exercise laid on by Group during a period of atrocious weather when the Sector Operations rooms were unlikely to be disturbed by the real enemy. Dummy raids were plotted all over the North of England and Southern Scotland. Group ordered off 602 and then 603. Meanwhile an elderly Flight Lieutenant, who had gained flying speed in the mess with the aid of a whisky bottle, assumed control of the battle in the

Turnhouse Sector Operations Room. His phone rang.

"Group Controller here. What are you doing about these raids – where is 602?" "On patrol at Auchenshuggle, Sir" replied the happy Sector Controller. (If it was not actually Auchenshuggle it was some other wee place near Glasgow.) After a pause, "What about 603?" "Angels 10, Sir, over Auchenshuggle." The Wing Commander at Group was beginning to fidget. "I'm scrambling 111 Squadron. This is a heavy raid where do you suggest we send them?" "Auchenshuggle, Sir," came the reply. "Why Auchenshuggle" demanded the Group Controller, "what's so special about it?" "Very important target, Sir." "What's that for heavens sake?" demanded the exasperated Group Controller. "It"s my house, Sir, I live there!"

Hopefully it was his last appearance at Turnhouse.

In contrast to those first months of the war Joe Bradfordís course founded on experience gained over the Low Countries and during the Battle of Britain was a real advance in our training programme. I was surprised by how much I had to learn.

Woodlands was a large three storey villa with a big lawn used to simulate the interception of enemy raids by fighter aircraft. This was performed by using specially adapted ice crean vender's tricycles fitted with RT to communicate with a student controller in the model sector operations room inside Woodlands house. These trikes were each fitted with a pilots compass and were ridden blind by the pupils on the course, with the view ahead and the side blocked by a large rather top heavy blinding shield attached round the front of the handle bars. In order to operate the equipment the pilot rider had to synchronise his pedalling in time with a metronome. This device consisted of a pendulum marked out like a ruler with air speeds given in miles per hour - low speeds at the bottom and high speeds at the top. The speed ordered by the operations room could be increased by sliding the boss weight up the pendulum to the appropriate reading. The pendulum ticked like a grandfather clock. One half turn on the pedals was required for each tick to give the correct air speed over the lawn.

Before the exercise began the bomber trikes were given secret instructions with regard to their courses and air speeds. The plotting table in the Operations Room was a scaled down map of the lawn. The relative positions of the raiders and the fighter trikes were plotted on the table as a result of bearings taken by airmen using telescopes mounted as simulated DF (direction finding) stations situated on the roof and in the garden. These visual bearings were passed by phone to the DF tables in the house with an airman on each string - just like the real thing. Another airman would tell the plot through to the Training

Operations Room. All this was to enable the student controller to direct his fighters to achieve an interception on the lawn outside. Mr Heath Robinson, the characterturist, would have loved it!

It was lectures in the morning and triking in the afternoon.

Unfortunately the designer of the trikes had not bargained for a rider with an artificial leg. Sure enough it got wedged between the pedal and the wooden shield with the result that the whole contraption keeled over and down it went on its side, together with its trapped pilot, onto the lawn. I was no doubt the only pilot who crashed at Woodlands. Joe Bradford took it in his stride. He bore me no ill will and returned me to Scotland for duty as a Sector Controller.

On my return to Scotland from Woodlands, I emerged from the underground station to find high explosive bombs and incendiaries raining down on Kings Cross and St Pancras railway stations. The enemy must have learned that a new Ace Controller was on his way back to Turnhouse! I hurried into the station and scrambled hastily on board the 10.00 pm from Kings Cross to Edinburgh, hoping for an early start, which took place with an enormous jolt about two minutes earlier than scheduled. As we cleared Kings Cross I saw the splendid arch over the railway shed in St Pancras Station still intact but festooned with incendiary bombs.

During my short stay at Turnhouse I had my first experience of a UFO (unidentified flying object). This was reported by the Observer Corps as an aircraft they could not identify somewhere between Kincardine and Alloa, with no apparent direction and without a reported height. I scrambled a section from 603 which was led by Flight Lieutenant Boulter, one of their Flight Commanders. The object was still reported visible from the ground but 603 could not see it, so after a while I sent them home, and then, I think, the daylight faded and the object disappeared.

I have seen three more of these UFOs since the war. On two occasions motoring home to Kilmacolm about twenty-five years ago there was a stationery light about four times as bright as Venus east of Formakin. The height was hard to judge in the dark - perhaps 4,000 feet. On both occasions it moved its position but not like an aircraft. My third sighting about 1992 was at night, I think, about two miles south of my bedroom window in Lochwinnoch Road, Kilmacolm. The height, as usual, was hard to judge, maybe 3,000 to 4,000 feet. It sat in much the same position for several nights and then it receded south to a new position before disappearing. None of these sightings could be accounted for by aircraft or balloons.

There has got to be an explanation; but what on earth is it?

Early in 1941 I was posted as a Controller to RAF Station Ayr, a new fighter base in the course of construction at the village of Heathfield near Ayr. The Station Commander, who was also the Sector Commander, was Wing Commander Loel Guiness, an Auxiliary Officer who had been in command of 601 County of London Squadron. In peacetime he was a merchant banker, whose legendary wealth was matched by his powerful personality and drive. The stories told about Guiness were already building him into a legend. It was said that when he came to Heathfield shortly before I arrived he found that everything had ground to a halt. When Loel confronted the contractors they complained that they had not had their money. The Air Ministry were dragging their feet. Guiness then asked them how much, and wrote them a cheque from his own account which he got back from the Air Ministry later on. Suddenly buildings appeared almost like magic!

The new fighter base at Heathfield proved to be both a sound tactical and strategic decision, although at the time it seemed to be a waste of money and effort with the splendid aerodrome at Prestwick already in use for fighter operations. Soon, however, the true strategic significance of Prestwick began to emerge. The Trans-Atlantic Control Centre was established in Redbrae, a large house across the road from Orangefield Hotel now inside the aerodrome. The aircraft from the United States began to arrive.

The new sector operations room responsible for the air defences of the west and north-west of Scotland was just coming on stream at Rosemount, a secluded country house about two miles up the Kilmarnock Road from the village of Monkton. The presiding genius under the Sector Commander was the Senior Controller, Sir Archibald Hope, Bart DFC, also an ex Auxiliary from 601 Squadron. We were soon joined by Huseph Riddle ex 601 and Francis Blackadder DSO, ex 607. We were promoted as Acting Squadron Leaders.

Despite this array of talent there was not much we could do when the night raids soon began on Clydeside. As Sector Commander Loel Guinness had by day 602 Squadron which was resting at Prestwick pending the completion of the airfield at Heathfield. For night defence we had 141 Squadron equipped with the Bolton and Paul Defiant, a make shift night fighter rather like an over sized Hurricane made for two, but much slowed down by a heavy gun turret in the back which mounted four Browning machine guns.

I was on watch when the raid developed over Clydebank and Greenock. Group ordered a "fighter night" by which a block of the atmosphere above the target area, and above a prescribed height, was allotted and reserved for the fighters; so we just sent all the night fighters we had. 602, who had been on day readyness, were already stood down. Some pilots including Sandy Johnstone, still in command, scrambled off over the target area, but got nothing better than a view of the bombs pelting down on Greenock and Clydebank!

I was glad when Loel Guiness and Archie Hope arrived up at Rosemount to take charge of this one sided battle which I knew I could not win. We had a large blackboard with a map of the sector waiting for such occasions. All we could do was depict the area where the raid was raging, so there was little more the Sector Commander or the Senior Controller could do. One lucky Defiant pilot caught a bomber in the moonlight broad side on which his gunner destroyed. Another was claimed by the anti-aircraft defences.

The raid must have been a disappointment for Squadron Leader Woolf commanding 141 Squadron. His Squadron had worked like blacks to be ready for something like this. I was sorry for them but much more sorry for Clydebank and Greenock!

Shortly after the Clydeside raids 602 moved across from Prestwick to the new fighter base at Heathfield. I seem to remember visiting Sandy Johnstone in Prestwick where he was confined to bed with a painful attack of mumps. His daughter was born there. In April 1941 Squadron Leader J I Kilmartin, OBE, DFC became Commanding Officer in succession to Sandy with the redoubtable Alan Deere, one of the Flight Commanders. We had an anxious moment in the Ops Room when Deere's engine seized up - an unusual occurrence for a Rolls-Royce Merlin. To our great relief he managed to land the Spitfire on the Heads of Ayr.

Squadron Leader P Meagher was in command of 602 Squadron from June to August 1941. I never met him.

Following the raids on Clydeside a visit was made to RAF Station Heathfield by the Major General in Command of the Third AA Division. His object was to inspect his anti-aircraft defences from the air; so off he went in the back seat of Squadron Leader Woolf's Defiant. Of course, it just had to happen. After weeks of enemy inactivity just when Woolf and his passenger had begun their inspection a hostile appeared on the table, somewhere near Lanark. To get more Defiants from Heathfield to reach operational height in time to be of any use would probably take fifteen minutes. That would be too late, so I decided to get one off for what it was worth, but in the meantime I ordered Woolf to intercept. Major Tommy Young, our AC/AC Liaison Officer (who later became the Sheriff at Linlithgow) was horrified. I had thrown his General into battle without consulting him. "Marvellous for the morale of his troops if he and Woolf get one" was my reply. Tommy was not impressed. Then I thought to myself - "I hope to God the GOC knows how to operate the gun turret and fire the Brownings. Well damn it all the man is a Gunner!" Of course, nothing came of it, and in due course they landed safely back at Heathfield. As soon as I knew they were down I phoned the General at the 141 dispersal. He was as pleased as punch with the whole business. I heaved a sigh of relief!

Just about this time there were was a significant improvement in the night fighting potential of Fighter Command. The Defiants were being phased out and replaced by the heavily armed Bristol Beaufighter powered by two huge radial engines which enabled it to outpace and catch most enemy bombers. The Defiants had already been practising with a new radar device known as AI (Air Interception). This was fitted into the navigator's compartment behind the pilot in the Beaufighter. Although I never had occasion to examine the equipment, it did, I believe, function by means of two display tubes; one for the navigator to guide the pilot to the height of the target, and the other for giving lateral adjustments to bring the fighter directly in line with its victim. The Beaufighter would then overhaul its prey. When the enemy exhaust flames began to show the pilot would open fire with his devastating armament. After that God help the enemy. Nothing else could.

The Beaufighter with its four cannons and six machine guns was in due course superseded by the De Havilland Mosquito, a light wooden twin engined aeroplane with a much greater overtaking speed. The comparatively flimsy the Mosquito packed four cannons firing forwards which was enough. The navigator could operate the AI sitting beside the pilot which was a great advantage.

The new AI equipment was just what we had been waiting for; but it would be of little use unless the controller on the ground could direct the fighter into a position behind, and sufficiently close, to bring it within AI radar range; moreover the fighter had to be close enough to avoid a long time-wasting stern chase. The answer came quite quickly in the form of a new device known as the GCI (Ground Control Interception).

In addition to the original CH Flood Light stations, as the war developed the coastal cover had been augmented by the Chain Home Low stations. The CHL, as it was called, was sited, if possible, on a cliff top from which the CHL transmitted a narrow beam from a horizontally revolving array which looked like a huge bed frame (see page 75). The operator would observe the course of beam in a circular display consul about twelve inches in diameter. The sparkling blue radar trace revolved in unison with the circulating aerial array outside. As the beam swept across an aircraft its echo appeared as a small smear in the shape of an arc - known as a "blip", which pulsed with its Cockerel for a friendly fighter.

The benefit of the CHL for the Filter Rooms was enormous, but the equipment was still incapable of reading under 500 feet. However, the principle of the revolving beam was soon adapted for the new GCI mobile control unit, which was probably the most important development of all.

The GCI swept round 360° to a range of about forty-five miles both over land and sea. The tube was etched with a map of the operational area of the set superimposed by the Fighter Command grid thus enabling the geographical Fighter Command grid co-ordinates of the echoes to be plotted. What mattered most was that we could at last see our fighters and their targets together in plan which resulted in a complete revolution in our controlling technique. From now on it would be possible to position the night fighter within AI range behind its target.

Apart from the area immediately surrounding the GCI station, which was swamped out by the pulse from the radar transmitter, the geographical Fighter Command grid positions of all plots could be told through on a plotting line to sector operations, thus supplementing the ROC (Royal Observer Corps) who could not see through cloud. Height finding was a problem with the GCI. Fortunately the ROC were able to give estimated heights.

To our surprise at Rosemount one of the earliest, if not the first operational GCI station, consisting of a convoy of mobile vehicles arrived at Prestwick, and was installed in a small field beside St Quivox Road.

Unlike the CHL which swept low over the sea the GCI could sweep all round to operational heights, but its beam had to be set above obstructions and high ground. Even so the mountains in the south of Ayrshire and Arran blotted out part of our operational field, but the coastal plain north and south of Prestwick proved to be good GCI coverage. Training in conjunction with 602 and 141 began at once. Despite its limitations the GCI was an enormous advance. The controller could actually see the echoes of the aircraft without having to worry about the time lags, and the inevitable errors of information arriving from various sources, resulting only in a guessed result, which could not be seen and checked.

Within the narrow confines of the GCI vehicle control by RT was exercised in darkness. The Controller with his small team consisting of airmen and airwomen and a technical officer, with a screwdriver at the ready, would sit like a fortune teller in a dark tent, gazing at the revolving trace in its 12 inch diameter consul, revealing in plan the relative position of the enemy and the fighter blips. The latter was identified by its pulsing IFF cockerel. To get the fighter at the right height, reasonably close behind the target, was an anxious and tricky operation requiring a lot of practice to get the knack of it.

During my first attempt I suddenly became aware of a sleeve at my elbow, adorned with one thick and two Flying Officer stripes. What I was doing was evidently so important that an Air Marshal had thought worthwhile to come and join the fun!

The GCI, as a satellite of the sector control room, called for additional controllers at Ayr. In consequence Squadron Leader W E Gemmell, Flight Lieutenants Lewin and Brogden were posted to Ayr sector. All three had been pilots in the Great War. Tiny Gemmell, an officer of vast proportions must have had difficulty in fitting into a Sopwith Camel or whatever he flew against Von Richthofenís circus. After the war he joined me as my No 2 in 3602 Fighter Control Unit of the Auxiliary Air Force which I raised in 1948.

Brogie from Dungannon in Ulster, still dressed in his uniform almost green with age from 1918, eventually joined my team as a Controller in Northern Ireland.

Following the raids on Clydeside we were briefly reinforced in the Ayr Sector by 600 Squadron recently equipped with the Beaufighter. I went down to see them land and taxi in under the leadership of the redoubtable and legendary George Stainforth, famous for his part in the Schnieder Trophy when he flew the Gloster Napier sea plane. He duly climbed down from his cockpit – a handsome figure nursing a Yorkshire terrier to his chest. I wondered if he took it with him on patrol to frighten the Germans! Stainforth's elder brother Moxon, who was married to my cousin Fiona MacLean, told me an amusing story about George as a boy in Yorkshire. A wasps' nest was discovered in the Stainforth garden which George and his friends decided to destroy. As they advanced on the target George was observed hanging back at the rear of the party. "What are you doing, George" demanded the leading boy. "I'm praying" was the reply! The story gives a clue to Stainforth's outstanding airmanship which combined caution and thorough preparation before undertaking hazardous experimental flying. In one of his books Neville Shute describes Stainforth undertaking a particularly dangerous test flight. He sat in the cockpit for nearly an hour contemplating the controls and working out exactly what he would do if the anticipated failure took place. It did and he survived. Sadly he ran out of luck later in the Middle East where he was killed in action.

The enemy having apparently lost interest in the Clyde 600 Squadron was soon withdrawn to a more active sphere of operations, leaving us to the care of Squadron Leader Woolf and his Defiants to do what they could by night. Eventually they were moved elsewhere and replaced by a squadron which was working up on Beaufighters under the

St Quivox GCI 1941
Approximate coverage superimposed on Fighter Grid

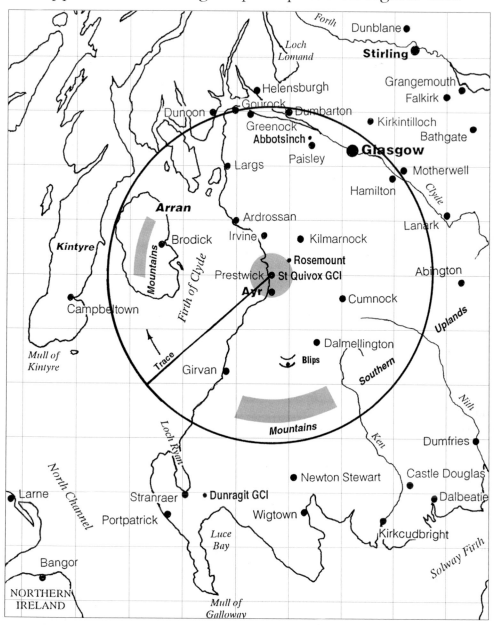

Showing revolving trace with blind spots over mountains and transmission pulse area. Also showing swept blips of a target flying north and a fighter in AI range with cockeril (IFF) flashing.

command of Wing Commander George Heycock. The new GCI site at Fullerton further up the coast improved the standard of Ground Control interception. Apart from that I became involved in a most unfortunate disaster. Two of their young officers went off in a Magister. The pilot evidently decided to enjoy some illegal low flying but misjudged his height. They crashed into a back street in Prestwick. The pilot was killed outright but luckily his passenger escaped with his life. After the wreckage had been removed and the gristly remains, including some of the pilot's brains, had been swept up I was ordered by Loel to conduct the investigation. This proved easy enough when I found the scoring made by the starboard wing tip on a parapet wall in front of one of the adjacent houses. This indicated a steep turn just above street level; but too low. My next port of call was to the sick quarters to interview the passenger. I seem to remember his name. It was, I think, Plt Off Benn, the son of a prominent labour peer. He was lucky to be alive.

Loel was duly promoted Group Captain and posted to Bentley Priory as Assistant to the C-in-C. He was succeeded as Station and Sector Commander by an agreeable and efficient regular Wing Commander. Unfortunately I cannot recall his name.

By this time 602 had departed in July 1941 to Kenley for a further tour of operations. The Sector continued as a so called place of rest for a number of day fighter squadrons, including 312 (Czech) Squadron complete with their own Controller, Flight Lieutenant Vrana, to cope with the language. They were followed by the Free French who arrived without an allotted RT call sign. "Poison" was immediately suggested, but fortunately for allied relations the Signals branch did not fall for that one! I was accorded the honour of an invitation to their dispersal to shake the hand of General de Gaulle when he visited the Squadron soon after their arrival. I was impressed. There was nothing stiff or proud about the General on that occasion. He mixed in with the officers and men who clearly thought the world of him. De Gaulle's brief visit did much to improve their moral.

Soon after this our own new Station Commander ran into a spot of bad luck. At the time we had at Heathfield (which became known as RAF Station Ayr) not only a day and a night fighter squadron; but also a squadron of Army Co-operation Command.

In the fullness of time the new Commander in Chief of Fighter Command, Air Chief Marshal Sir Sholto Douglas, decided to pay us a visit. The whole place was smartened up and every effort made in preparation for such an important occasion. The troops were to line each side of the roadway from the gate to station headquarters, complete, I believe, with buglers, and all pomps and ceremonies appropriate for a C & C's inspection. Those of us not on watch or at readyness were summoned to the mess to greet the great man and have lunch with him; but when I arrived to my surprise there was a tense frosty atmosphere in the crowded ante-room with embarrassed tongue-tied officers standing around in little groups. In a chair facing the stove sat a portly figure with one thick and three ordinary rings on his sleeve reading a newspaper with his back to the assembled company.

I heard the explanation later. All had been ready and set by 10.50 hours or earlier for Sholto's estimated time of arrival (ETA) at 11.00 am At five to eleven a large staff car flying an Air Marshal's flag rolled through the gates. The troops snapped to attention and presented arms. The show went into action and the CO dashed to the door of Station Headquarters to greet his guest. When the door of the car was opened the Goering like figure of Sir Sholto was not revealed, but out stepped an Air Marshal known, I believe, in the service as "Ugly" Barret, Commander-in-Chief of Army Co-operation Command who had made an unscheduled surprise visit to his Squadron. No sooner was "Ugly" on his way than yet another large staff car flying an Air Chief Marshal's flag rolled up to the aerodrome gate. It may even have been challenged by the bemused sentry, but it was too late – the show was over, the trap sprung and the troops dismissed leaving the unfortunate CO to face the music. Unfortunately the Commander-in-Chief failed to see the joke.

On 10th May 1941, a while before the Commander-in-Chief's visit the Ayr sector became briefly involved in one of the strangest events of the Second World War. 602 Squadron were not called upon to play an active role in the arrival of the Deputy Fuhrer, but their erstwhile Commanding Officer, Wing Commander His Grace the Duke of Hamilton had the misfortune to become involved in it, and I was the Sector Controller on duty at the time.

During the six to midnight watch, about half past ten, to my surprise a "hostile" appeared on our plotting table in the vicinity of Selkirk flying the west. The Ops Room sprang into action. Fortunately we had two Defiants fully armed airborne practising with their AI. I got them on the RT and told them to orbit Kilmarnock which seemed to lie in the path of the hostile.

I then phoned the Controller of the Royal Observer Corps centre in Ayr and asked if he had an identification. To my surprise he answered "Yes, it is an Me110". My heart sank - another cock-up for sure. "Better tell your chaps to have another look" I said. "If it's an Me110 it does not have enough petrol to get back to Germany." This was a tricky situation for the Controller, I had to warn the Defiants that doubt had arisen whether it was hostile. There was very little ROC cover over the Southern Uplands. The night was falling fast. No further plots appeared and no further sightings were reported. Foiled again!

About an hour later the phone buzzed. Ops B answered. "It's a Police Sergeant wants to speak to you Sir, from Eaglesham Police Station, I think", he said. What an extraordinary evening! "Yes Sergeant what is it?" "We have a German Captain here at the police station, he has landed by parachute. He says he wants to see the Duke of Hamilton." "That's odd, can he identify himself." "No Sir, he wont say any more." "All right Sergeant I will deal with it. We'll let you know".

As it turned out His Grace combined the duties of Station Commander at RAF Turnhouse with the operational role of Sector Commander for the defence of the eastern half of Scotland.

I got through to my opposite number in the Control Room at Turnhouse and asked to be put through to the Duke. I encountered a certain amount of opposition. The CO has gone for the night. "Where has he gone?" "He has a house on the station". "I must be put through at once". A voice answered from the Duke's house, maybe it was the butler. He was reluctant to reveal His Grace's movements. He hesitated and then admitted that he had gone to bed.

"Well you'll have to get him up. Tell him Squadron Leader Hector MacLean is on the line and it's urgent". A few minutes later a rather tetchy voice answered. It was my erstwhile Commanding Officer. "What's all this Hector?" "A German Captain has parachuted from an Me110. He's at Eaglesham Police Station and wants to see you". Douglo was obviously nonplussed. "What does he want to see me about" he asked. "He wont say" I answered. Then after a pause. "What do you think I should do about it?" said the Duke. "I think you should go and see him". "Yes, I think I will". He put the phone down and I told Ops B to warn the Police he was coming.

I do not suggest for a moment that Douglo, an experienced Senior Officer, was in need of my advice, but he certainly needed time to think; and was obviously just as taken aback by this strange development as I was.

I recently heard Hess's account of his last moments in what must have been a frantic search for the closed down landing field at Dungavel. Sandy Johnstone, who had just been posted to Turnhouse became involved. The story he had heard was that the fellow calling himself Alfred Horn had mistaken the Defiants for Hurricanes when he caught sight of them climbing to intercept and had decided to bail out before they could draw a bead on him. Apparently Hess had been travelling downhill from a great height over the North Sea and, had therefore, easily been able to give the slip to the Spitfires based on the East Coast. He was already now beginning to look around for Dungavel where he intended to land. His subsequent reaction at sighting what he took to be Hurricanes was therefore understandable.

At the time I wish I had known this at Rosemount. A successful interception on the basis of one plot at a range of about seventy miles would have been a boost for our morale at Ops, and for the Observer Corps who had, in fact, distinguished themselves.

So began this extraordinary incident and a trial which eventually led to the imprisonment and death of Hess in Spandau jail.

On 5th May 1991 an article appeared in the Daily Telegraph suggesting that Hess had been deliberately let in, and that an RT Operator named Bryant remembered a message that the aircraft concerned was not to be attacked. To let Hess in by arrangement could only have been done with the connivance and co-operation of the Duty Controllers of Turnhouse and the Ouston sectors and myself at Ayr. To ignore a hostile or an unidentified X raid could only have been done on the order of the Wing Commander Group Controller at 13 Group Newcastle-on-Tyne. He himself would have to get an order of that kind from his AOC, Air Vice-Marshal Jock Andrews, or his SASO (Senior Air Staff Officer), or from the Duty Air Commodore at Fighter Command.

As already explained the Movement Liaison sections attached to each Filter Room were told about aircraft movements over the North Sea. It required experience and judgement on the part of the Filter Controller to make his identification by correlating aircraft movements with the mass of radar information streaming in from the various coastal stations. Frequently identifications had to be altered from hostile to friendly or vice versa as matters developed, nor did it help when the plot faded as it frequently did near the coast.

The foregoing account of the approach by Hess towards the Northumberland coast points to a classic situation for an Ogo Pogo (see pages 74/75). A change of identification would immediately appear on the Group and Sector Operations tables, perhaps long before the aircraft reached the coast. Our table at Ayr did not reach over the North Sea. Assuming this mysterious RT message was really transmitted it could well be explained by a quite proper reaction of the Sector Controller involved. Shooting down our own chaps was just as bad, if not worse, than shooting down Huns.

A temporary change in identification could, therefore, explain the R.T. message Bryant claims to have heard. It might just explain why Turnhouse, to whom we had a liaison line, never bothered to tell us what was going on over the North Sea; but that, of course, could also be explained by a lack of imagination on the part of the airman manning their liaison line position. To be fair, Turnhouse probably did not know that we had no liaison link to Ouston although we did have a line to Group. At a later date we were paid a visit by our new AOC, Air Vice-Marshal Jock Andrews. I asked him for a liaison line to Ouston. "Nonsense" he replied. "You'll be asking for a line to Rommel next, but you will have to wait till I get mine. He seems to be the only man who knows what is going on in this war". Jock had to have his little joke!

Apart from all that it was fortunate that by chance we had fighters on patrol with my orders to destroy the 110 which puts an end to any further speculation on the subject.

Winston Churchill's final verdict on the Hess affair is contained in Volume III of his History of the Second World War. It reads as follows.

"Reflecting upon the whole of this story I am glad not to be responsible for the way in which Hess was being treated. Whatever may be the moral guilt of a German who stood near Hitler, Hess had, in my view atoned for this by his completely devoted and frantic deed of lunatic benevolence. He came to us of his own free will and, though without authority, had something of the quality of an envoy. He was a medical not a criminal case and should have been so regarded."

That seemed to be the end of the matter. Hess's arrival soon became public knowledge. I received no security briefing at the time but did not reveal any details outside the Service until after the war was over. The matter was known about and logged in the Ops Room at the time, although the Rosemount logbook has, I understand, been lost. My account of the incident was published many years ago in the RAF Association's magazine "Air Mail". So if the details I have repeated were ever supposed to be secret they certainly are secret no longer. About five years ago at the request of the Imperial War Museum I gave their representative a taped interview about my war time memories. They agreed to let me have a duplicate tape which duly arrived from London. Much to my surprise the tape came suddenly to an abrupt end when I began my description of Hess's arrival. This has made me wonder whether there is someone in authority, either with instructions or acting on his or her own initiative, who is giving orders to keep the lid on information connected with the Hess affair. If so it is high time that the lid was taken off. Should there still be an unrevealed secret the British people, and particularly those of us who spent six years of our young lives containing the aspirations of the German tyranny, have a right to know it.

In the spring of 1941 my first wife and I were married in Westbourne Church, Glasgow. Donald Jack was my best man. After that we settled at 35 Gray Street, Prestwick which had to be given up in time for our eldest son Donald to be born at Dulnain Bridge; but by this time I had been posted to Belfast.

Apart from controlling at Rosemount, and at the GCI I was, during my later months at the Ayr sector, detailed to organise a training course for the increasing number of Fighter Controllers who would be needed for future offensive operations. Tiny Gemmell acted as my assistant professor! The young penguin officers, as they were rather rudely called, came from a variety of civilian background employments. As far as we could judge they had been selected by some IQ test; but without operational flying experience would they have the necessary authority, personality or common sense for coping with situations as they arose? They sat in by turns on watch at Rosemount and I organised lectures to cover the theory. A small proportion were clearly unsuitable and had to be weeded out, but would the remainder make the grade in practise? During my watch one of my pupils reported a "rat warning" from Machrihanish. Even Windy Joe's course at Woodlands had not prepared me for that one!

After much thought I decided on a written examination followed by an oral test as adopted by the legal faculty for examining their degree students at the University of Glasgow. Each candidate was examined in turn on a series of imaginary crisis situations. I will never forget the reaction of one embryo controller. We simulated a call on the R.T. from a Spitfire plotted at the Cock of Arran where the Glasgow sewage is dumped. "I am on fire" said the pilot. After a pause our likely lad gave him a vector of about 230° magnetic (SW) whereas it should have been, say, 100° magnetic (east). He should have asked the aircraft's height. Moreover he failed to warn the Air Sea Rescue Services and tell the pilot he had done so. "Why 230° magnetic"? we asked. "To land him at Limavady" (near Londonderry) was his reply. "Why Limavady?" "It is quite close" said he. Then the penny dropped. He had been sitting for two months staring at a huge map of the Clyde estuary and was under the impression that the island of Arran was Ireland. He would have had a problem getting the blazing Spitfire down at Lochranza!

Fortunately most of the other students passed and went on to play their part in the air war.

A lack of grounding in geography and an inability to map read was not confined to my students at Ayr.   Later in the war I had occasion to visit a department concerned with radar coverage at Air Ministry Bush House.   I can't remember the exact problem which was worrying the two English Flight Lieutenants in charge, but my solution was simple – "You have a radar station in Shetland".   "And where is that" they replied.   "A hundred and fifty miles north of Aberdeen" I replied.   "Oh yes" said one of them.   "Now I remember; at school it was in a box opposite Aberdeen!"

The war had not gone well in 1941, but on 7th December the whole scene suddenly changed when the Japanese launched their devastating attack on Pearl Harbour.   Things began to look ugly for us in the Far East.   Indeed they proved to be worse than expected; but most of us sighed with relief.   The Americans were in at last.   For the first time we could see light far away at the end of the tunnel.   Bismarck's strategic assessment would ultimately prove Hitler's undoing.

35 Gray Street, Prestwick, within walking distance of the GCI at St Quivox Road, was a pleasant and restful change from the traumatic events of 1939 and 1940.

One morning in the autumn of 1941 Marcia woke up to find she had turned bright red from top to toe.   In haste I summoned the young Squadron Leader M.O. from Heathfield. "Good God" he exclaimed as I opened the bedroom door and he beheld his patient.   After recovering from the initial shock he diagnosed German Measles.   Fortunately our elder son William Donald MacLean was born without ill effects on 29th May 1942.

I had never been able to convince my first wife about the atrocities that were being perpetrated by the Nazis against the Jews.   She still believed, like many others, that Nazi genocide was part of our wartime propaganda.   But it was all too true as I was able to demonstrate later during our sojourn at Belmont Road, in Belfast.   On that occasion the very same American magazine which had introduced me to Hitler during my schooldays published a set of detailed photographs smuggled out of an extermination camp in Poland. One picture was taken of the roof above the extermination chamber with a stub chimney for the executioners to pour down cyanide upon the victims herded in below.   The second photograph showed the actual drums of cyanide waiting in store, and the third a line of crude log fired ovens needed to complete the disposal of the human remains.   Those pictures should have been dropped all over Germany.

No wonder Winston Churchill demanded unconditional surrender.   Nothing less would do.

CHAPTER 13
AIRSTAFF

Most of the raiders which came to Clydeside arrived from the east, but some came via the Irish Sea which we had expected them to do. To meet that threat Fighter Command had established an additional GCI for the Ayr sector at Dunragit, a satellite of RAF Station West Freuch near Stranraer. Dunragit did not get much trade, but the wily Hun arrived in considerable force up the Irish Sea and turned left giving Belfast a pasting. The loyal citizens of the Province complained, and their provincial government at Stormont was displeased. Fighter Command rose to the occasion and gave Ulster the full treatment. 82 Fighter Group was established in the building at Stormont with a Group Operations room in the Senate Chamber. Sector Operations Rooms were built in the Fighter Command stations at Ballyhalbert in County Down, St Angelo by Lough Earn, and Eglinton near Londonderry. No less than four GCI stations were established at suitable technical locations in the province. A new Filter Room was established at Dundonald in Belfast together with coastal radar stations sited as far north as Islay. No doubt all this soon became known to the enemy who probably concluded that their aircraft could be more profitably employed elsewhere. They rarely, if ever, came again to Northern Ireland.

In retrospect this may seem to have been an expensive diversion of equipment and manpower, but there was a hidden strategic possibility that the enemy might invade and occupy Southern Ireland which could scarcely defend itself. The army were, in fact, building up a force in Ulster, and making plans to deal with such a situation. An army ghost division known as BTNI was held in reserve somewhere near Lisburn.

In the meantime a staff officer was required to take charge of the control and reporting empire. Squadron Leader (Sally) Sarel, a South African who was regarded as the ace control and reporting expert, was to take charge. I think he must have had friends at Court. He may have advised on the set up, but he never returned to see it in action. No doubt, in desperation, they posted me to 82 Group to take charge under the supervision of the SASO Group Captain (Minnie) Manton. This was not our family's first involvement in Northern Ireland. When he came down from Cambridge my brother, Bruce MacLean, joined the army and was initially employed in the field security in Ulster before being commissioned into the

Argyll & Sutherland Highlanders, and later transferred to the Black Watch. Bruce's task was to play the part of a simple soldier, mixing with the local population, drinking Guiness, gathering information and watching for subversion.

Even in 1942 sabotage was a real problem in Ulster. I remember the IRA giving us some entertainment for which we had a ringside seat in the Control Room at Stormont. An Avro Anson with a crew of pupils from Jurby in the Isle of Man, without RT, had got itself well and truly lost at night over Eire. We were plotting it wandering around south of the border, but were powerless to do anything for them. In the meantime the IRA had decided to strike a blow at the hated British, so by night they managed to get into Cluntoe Richardson on the west side of Loch Neagh. This was a big new airfield under construction and almost ready for the reception of American B-17 Flying Fortresses. The raiders then began to build and light a huge bonfire on the main runway. To our relief the luckless Anson finally turned north across the border and then headed in the direction of Loch Neagh. Soon we heard they had seen the fires and made a successful landing at Cluntoe. A very Irish result.

At Stormont the air staff consisting of Evone Kirkpatrick ex-603 with his spiky moustache, Jack Riddle ex-601 preparing and patiently waiting for the enemy to invade Southern Ireland, and myself in charge of the control operating system, all sat together in one of the ceremonial robing rooms for the Senate. As time went by it became clear that we were overmanned for our role and I became progressively involved (with some relish as a taxpayer) in the amalgamation and concentration of our establishments, releasing more and more personnel for overseas operations and, hopefully, for the second front. The proportion of WAAF personnel continued to increase. There must have been about five hundred women in the control and reporting organisation, all strictly out of bounds for officers in uniform and for us married men; though some fell by the wayside!

I enjoyed the first six months of my staff appointment at Stormont where we came directly under the Senior Air Staff Officer (the SASO) Group Captain G A L Manton, a regular officer sometimes unjustly referred to as "Moaning Minnie". He wisely allowed me just enough rein to sort all kinds of problems which arose almost daily from the operation and manning of our considerable control and reporting empire. It was a novel experience quite different from operational flying and controlling. The most enjoyable, and a very important part of the work, was visiting the stations and units under our command which we always did, where possible, by air using our own communications flight aeroplanes at Sydenham.

The command under the AOC was divided between the SASO and the Senior Officer of

Organisation – the SOA, who both reported directly to him.

Organisation ("Org") consisted of a host of supportive activities including personnel ("P Staff"), Equipment, Accounts, Catering, Education, and works and bricks.

The SOA was also responsible for the Command Headquarters unit which included Transport, Accommodation billeting and the officers mess at Ardtullagh. The HQ unit was under the command of Wing Commander Evone Kirkpatrick ex-603 Squadron who, as Air 1, was also responsible for the communications flight at Sydenham.

As I remember it the three Fighter Command stations at Ballyhalbert, Eglinton, St Angelo and the four GCIs came under RAFNI for their ground organisation and support. The same applied Long Kesh, Newtonards and the four GCIs, and to a lesser extent the Coastal Command stations at Ballykelly, Limavaddy and Castle Archdale – Ballywooden GCI were lodgers on the Training Command Station at Bishops Court.

Air staff under the SASO, who were general duties officers with operational experience in the squadrons, were responsible for the Command's military part in the war for which we were supported and advised by separate specialist branches including the Medical branch, Anti Aircraft Liaison (AALO), Signals, Armament, Intelligence, Training, Air Raid Warnings, Security and Airfield Defence. Only the SASO had access to the AOC who, presumably, was left largely undisturbed to think his great thoughts! I was only summoned to the presence about twice during my prolonged sojourn in Northern Ireland. This was, of course, inherent in the system, but one tended to feel a bit left out of it. And that added to frustration.

The operational side of the Control and Reporting organisation, for which I was responsible, was heavily dependent on the telephone and this brought me into frequent contact with the Signals branch including Mr F J DeCourcey, an electronic engineer, who was our GPO Liaison Officer. As a result of these contacts it soon began to dawn on me that the ground control of air defences depended far more on communications than the actual location of the control rooms. Like all roads which lead to Rome all telephone lines led to Belfast so, in theory, there was no need for more than one Fighter Operations Room in Northern Ireland ñ and that is what, in the end, we managed to bring about; although we continued to maintain the Sector Operations Room at Ballyhalbert in working condition as a standby in case the Stormont building was destroyed by enemy attack. Without the Filter Room we could scarcely function. It was secreted unobtrusively in a Belfast school building. When I arrived it was under the command of Wing Commander Rose, a builder by trade who was soon succeeded by Wing Commander Gurney Fry, a London stockbroker. Both were real specialists in this new bizarre art. Without their assistance it would have been difficult for me to get to grips with the situation. My main worry was that one single bomb on the Dundonald Filter Room, which should have under ground, might wreck the whole organisation. I was also haunted by the prospect of a bomb on the Senate chamber at the Stormont. With my signals friends the GPO we had made plans for that; but there would be political side effects.

Rachael Hutchesson

Without the benefit of a staff college course it took me quite a while to get the hang of it all, and considerably longer to appreciate the pitfalls and weaknesses of the system which frequently resulted in delay and frustration for the staff, and those on the stations awaiting replies. The specialist branches had to be consulted where the problem concerned their organisation or needed their advice. A file on the subject would frequently pass down from the SASO to Air Staff, and then via the central registry of files to the branches concerned for their input. At that stage it might well be chewed over by one or more officers before coming back again via Air Staff to the SASO for action. It was, I suppose, a microcosm of the Air Ministry in London (rudely known as "The House of Shame!") If a project lay beyond our tight financial limits to "The House of Shame" it had to go, where some of the branches concerned might even be in different buildings in London all tholed to a mighty central registry which took charge each time the file moved. In simple cases I just put the file under my arm and went round the branches for their input, which usually was "Get on with it for God's sake" and so it would be ready for the SASO by lunch time – not three weeks later. I was never caught by Org!.

Soon after my posting to 82 Fighter Group at Stormont in Belfast we took over the whole of the RAF administration in Northern Ireland to be known as RAFNI which administered the RAF's presence in the province together with the Group Operations Room in the Senate Chamber in the Parliament Building. Our new AOC Air Vice Marshal Cole DSO MC (Old King Cole, as he soon became known), took over the command. He was a distinguished Australian veteran pilot from the Great War, and was by no means one of Norman Stone's swivel chair Air Marshals! The Dieppe raid had found him on the bridge of the vessel specially adapted and fitted out as a Fighter Control ship. Things began to hot up and the ship was attacked; Fighter Command's representative receiving a piece of shrapnel through his jaw. After a spell in hospital Cole was given a DSO and let lose on Northern Ireland where, in the absence of any Germans, he did his best to brighten up the social scene in Belfast until such time as the enemy might venture an invasion of Eire.

My turn soon came in the bar of the comfortable mess at Ardtullagh which we had taken over from the local golf club in Holywood. After a hard day pushing files into my out tray at Stormont I was having a convivial dram with our young southern Irish doctor when the AOC made his appearance like the ancient mariner amongst the wedding guests. We were duly selected to be his chaperones while he escorted Lady Duffryn to the 400 Club in Belfast, His Lordship being otherwise occupied elsewhere on National Service. So off we drove to pick up the Marchioness in a large Humber with the AOC's flag flying. On arrival we found our guest still putting on the final touches to her appearance. 'Old King Cole' was in cracking form and gave me a squish of her delicious, but very expensive perfume, an indiscretion for which he was roundly rebuked. Despite this lapse off we went in the Humber to find the entrance to the 400 Club blocked by a queue of merry makers lining the stairs which led up from the pavement to the doors of the establishment. I was at a loss as to how I could get the old man and his guest into the 400 Club without causing an incident or loss of face. In my long experience as a chaperone I had never encountered such a problem. The young Irish doctor took the matter out of my hands. "Make way" he yelled up the stairs, "Make way, we are technicians". It worked like a charm, the queue squeezed back in reverence against the wall and the AOC of Northern Ireland, with his party, made their dignified entrance into the Club. It must have been the first time Lady Duffryn had been described as a technician! I cannot remember much more about that evening that except that 'Old Bushmills' and "VAT 69' came into it.

The next morning I struggled along the corridor to answer the SASO's summons. "How did you get on" demanded Minnie. "How did you know about it Sir" I asked. "Ha, ha," he replied "I saw it coming, slipped out of the mess before I was lurked!"

'Old King Cole' got his own back on him when Minnie emigrated to Australia, having retired as a Group Captain. He was welcomed by Cole and a tail of Australian pals. They made short work of him. He was put to bed after the festivities.

As Air III with responsibility for the manning and operation of the Group Operations Room and the three Sector Operations Rooms and four GCI and a Filter Room I was the busiest man on the air staff at RAFNI, which suited me well because taking responsibility was just I wanted. Although Minnie Manton was sitting on my head he gave me just enough rope to get the job done. This was just as well because frustration was a very real disease among junior staff officers.

For want of a better metaphor, I would describe the RAF system as a group of administrative cones. The senior officer in each branch might have two or more officers of varying ability in his department. Some wanted to take responsibility and some did not. In every group there would be doers who would innovate and get things done, and 'no men' who usually outnumbered them, and either, by lassitude or by their very nature, managed to obstruct. If the senior officer himself was a 'no man' you needed dynamite!

Fortunately Minnie Manton was by no means a 'no man'. As a Squadron Commander in the Battle of Britain he had quelled an incipient mutiny which he discovered during a temporary visit by his Squadron to Manston. As an Acting Group Captain at RAFNI, where the pace was slower, Minnie veered towards caution. After taking our advice he would test our opinion by assuming the role of devil's advocate which frequently resulted in his winning the argument. On one or two occasions a question of some importance arose and, which in the opinion of Jack Riddle and myself, just had to have the right answer, and called for an argument we just could not afford to lose. We duly submitted the opposite solution which Minnie had little difficulty in rejecting. He must have thought what fools we were.

When he came to Heathfield Loel Guiness appeared to have mastered the art of dealing with "doers" and "no men" by bringing his own team. This included Archie Hope, a real doer, for operations and a squadron leader administration, who was by nature a no man, well able to filter out and refuse all but the best ideas for Loel's attention. These Loel would adopt, thereby advancing the war effort and enhancing his reputation as a man to get results, and also saved him from the pain of saying 'no'.

The personnel manning for the Control and Reporting organisation demanded continuous attention. To those coming in from civilian occupations the work was a novel experience which called for adaptability and a broad background education, rather than specialised work qualifications. For example, the wider range of subjects covered by the Scottish education system was probably more suitable than the narrower group of subjects selected for early specialisation by English schools. It used to be said with a grain of truth that the brightest WAAFs were those who had just been 'cocktail trained' since leaving school!

Our Senior Controller, Wing Commander George Knox, knew everybody and was always ready with his advice. Like the Duke of Plazatoro he was keen to promote all my people to the top of every tree, but I had to be more cautious. What went up rarely came down, which was awkward if you promoted a dud!

During 1942 we set up house in Belmont Road, Belfast, but my wife Marcia did not like Belfast so returned to Dulnain Bridge during 1943 where my second son, Marcus, was born on 24th January 1944. During the remainder of my time in Northern Ireland I lived in the Mess except for a brief time when I shared a house with George Knox. His wife, Dame Jean Knox, was a Chief Commandant of the ATS, but unfortunately the marriage was breaking down.

As the war developed our overseas operations called for more and more men, but getting them out of home based establishments such as RAFNI was like getting blood out of a stone; but something I was determined to do. Fortunately my chief mentor was Wing Commander John Cherry an auxiliary officer ex-600 Squadron who was Ops 2 at Fighter Command, and responsible to Air Staff there for the Control and Reporting System.

The Royal Observer Corps did not operate in Northern Ireland so we had to rely overland on our four GCIs, and on a number of visual observation posts manned by RAF personnel. These were sited around the coast preferably at points with telephone communication. Unfortunately some of the posts were beyond reach of the GPO and had to be manned by a detachment of the Wireless Observer Wing, (WOW), known as the 'Woo'. These airmen did their best reporting to the Filter Room in Morse code, but the inevitable time lag was so great that the next plot at the Filter Room received from other sources would appear before the first one from the Woo. In consequence the plot on the Ops table would go into reverse and then suddenly reappear about twenty miles further on in the original direction. I was not sorry when the Woo were withdrawn, particularly as they had obvious potential for overseas operations where the RAF would not have the benefit of land line communications.

After studying the set up in Northern Ireland the penny soon began to drop. As already mentioned the telephone was the key to the business, so the location of the control function basically depended on the telephone communications in the province which was centred in Belfast. John Cherry and his assistant, Squadron Leader Bob Foley another auxiliary, must have come to the same conclusion which led to the closing down of the Sector Operations Rooms at St Angelo, Eglington and Ballyhalbert, leaving us with a combined Group Sector Ops Room in the Senate Chamber at Stormont. The four GCIs were retained at Ballywooden,

Balydonachy, Lisnaskea and Ballinderry. The last mentioned GCI was situated on the west side of Lough Neagh in the heart of reputed IRA country. This prompted me to arrange a surprise visit to check the security. Together with Colonel Dillon, our staff officer in charge of station defence, we duly arrived at the pub beside Ballinderry Bridge and decided to have a preliminary glass of Guiness before proceeding to the GCI Station. "You will be visiting Ballinderry?" asked the Landlord. It was an awkward question but there was no use pretending. "Well, yes, we were thinking of it". "Well now" said our host, "You'll be wasting your time there. That station is closed for quarterly maintenance". So much for our deadly secret! Fortunately for the RAF the IRA were not quite so active in those days.

During 1943 Flight Officer Rachael M Hutchesson came to HQ RAFNI to be one of our Ops B officers at Stormont. She had volunteered in March 1940 and was reputed the fastest plotter in C Watch down the hole at Bentley Priory, where she became the only WAAF known to have assaulted the Commander in Chief. Blissfully unaware that Stuffy was prowling round the plotting floor Corporal Hutchesson achieved one of her lightening plots and withdrew her long magnetic aluminium rod so sharply that she took the Air Chief Marshal by surprise fair and square in his midriff. It was probably the only wound he received during his war, but I doubt if he qualified for a wound stripe! He was not so fortunate a year or so later when, as Inspector General of the RAF, he is reported to have got his trousers burned while walking too close behind the exhaust of an experimental jet aircraft.

In the meantime the ace plotter had fallen from grace. Fighter Command was responsible for the safety of His Royal Highness the Duke of Kent who was being flown in secrecy on some important mission. His plot on the Fighter Command table was awaited but at the expected time it did not appear. At the crucial moment the attention of the duty Air Commodore was drawn to a friendly plot in a completely different fifty mile grid square. He refused to believe it. Corporal Hutchesson was the tops. The truth was soon revealed; she had managed to lose His Majesty's younger brother! Fortunately the Duke reached his destination in safety, but was their ace plotter over the hill? Apparently not because soon after she was commissioned and subsequently appointed as an Air Raid Warning Officer at the 10 Group operations room, with authority to wail bad news into every home and corner in the South West of England.

Flight Officer Hutchesson's arrival at Stormont many months later to fill an Ops B post established for a Section Officer called for a reduction in rank. This caused me some embarrassment.   To my surprise the loss of her second stripe did not seem to worry her. Later on I was equally surprised to hear that she continued to get the pay of a Flight Officer, which seemed to explain the matter.

After the war Rachael Hutchesson, who was trained as a Norland nurse, became the matron of the RAF home at Rooks Hill near Sevenoaks established to take care of children who had lost their fathers in the war.   In 1949 she gave it up and married me on 4th June of that year.   She continues to give complete satisfaction in her final posting!

Despite the fact that Eire was neutral and complete with a German Embassy in Dublin, the proportion of their young men who had volunteered to join our fighting services was high, if not higher, than from Ulster. When Eire became an independent nation Great Britain had wisely reserved the use of two naval bases on the West Coast of Eire. Despite the fact that German 'U' boats had almost brought us to the brink of defeat in the Great War, a later British Government in a moment of strategic lunacy relinquished our rights to these bases which would have been of such value to the Royal Navy in their struggle against the 'U' boats in the Battle of the Atlantic. For Eire to have allowed us the use of these bases would have been regarded by Hitler as an act of war.

Although Eire permitted her citizens to volunteer the best they could do for our air forces was to allow our aircraft to cross over the narrow strip of their land beyond Belleek in Eire. This gave coastal command and, in particular our Short Sunderland flying boats, direct access to the Atlantic from their base at Castle Archdale in Lough Erne without having to trudge all the way round the north coast of Donegal.

Another important concession was made. In order to build up the United States Air Force it was essential to get their B-24 Liberators and B-17 Flying Fortresses safely over the Atlantic and then lead them down to the bases prepared for them in Ulster, after making their landfall, over the west coast of Ireland. To have these valuable aircraft wandering round Eire after their gruelling flights across the ocean, would have been almost as embarrassing for the British and the Irish Governments as for the exhausted air crews themselves.

To their credit the Southern Irish Government agreed to a simple but diplomatically hazardous solution whereby large placards were erected and maintained at remote points down the whole of the Atlantic coast of Eire. Each placard was painted with a large number clearly visible from the air. Each point, and its number marked on a secret map, was carried in the aircraft. After making his landfall all the pilot had to do was fly along the Irish coast till a number came into view. He would then get his fix and find his way to Prestwick or

Group/Sector Ops – Senate Chamber, Stormont, Belfast
AA Guns Liaison   Air Staff
Ops B - S/O Hutchesson
Controller - Sqn Ldr Endersby
GCI Liaison   Deputy Controller   Dead Reckoning

through the Belleek corridor into Ulster. Soon the Transatlantic reinforcements (the "Transats") were flowing into Prestwick and the bases we had built for their reception in Northern Ireland.

From our headquarters we often had to send out questionnaires to units which frequently produced ambiguous and inaccurate answers, or no answers at all! This was mainly due to the lack of plain language and the sloppy ambiguous way the questions were asked. It is a malaise which still haunts modern burocracy. I eventually found the answer which was to try the questionnaire out on someone without any specialised knowledge, and without the enthusiasm of the sender. I recommend this solution.

By 1943 the stump of my right leg had still failed to heal. A re-amputation was advised, and carried out at the RAF hospital Halton by a Liverpool surgeon Air Commodore Osmond Clark. It was painful but nothing like it was after the original destruction of the limb, although it did not stop the burning in my phantom foot. This had done little to improve my temper in the office.

There was an interesting story current in our ward at Halton concerning a separate group of about five officer patients suffering from nothing else but frustration. Presumably they were baffled "yes men"! More riveting was the story of our young Canadian colleague. He had been shot down with a silver cigarette case in his trouser pocket. On bailing out, when he pulled the buckle his straps drove the case into his groin with the full force of the opening parachute. He was admitted in agony to hospital where the doctors advised immediate dissection of his private parts. He refused this treatment. "Then you will die" replied the docs. "I don't care" was his rejoinder. The MOs put their heads together and told him they would do what they could to save the working parts; but could he trust them? On waking up from the chloroform he found himself to be intact, but he still doubted if he was truly potent, so with regret he wrote a letter to his fiancée breaking off their engagement. However, a few weeks later on waking up he experienced an erection. This important development he communicated to the young nursing sister in charge of his case. She reacted beyond the call of duty. When he was good and ready she took him to one of the empty side wards for Wing Commanders and above, where his equipment was successfully tried out! Hastily he wrote to his fiancée asking to be taken back. As I was leaving the ward the good news came that all was to be well. It was not exactly a case for an award of an OBE but I rather think the young sister earned one!

About three weeks after Osmond Clark's surgery I had my first fitting for a new leg at

Roehampton, a highly efficient establishment which fitted limbs for amputees from all three services including Great War veterans with whom one could compare notes and get valuable tips. I made a few trips to London from Northern Ireland for fittings at Roehampton until my file was sent to the newly established limb centre at Belfast (Irish legs for Irish stumps!). There I was fitted with my second leg which was so badly done that in one day it produced an inflamed nerve end known as 'neuroma', which would have to be dug out at RAF Hospital Church Village in South Wales. Fortunately I was able to fly to an aerodrome near Cardiff in one of our Oxfords which the communications flight pilot flew back to Sydenham. Ten days later I flew the Oxford back the same way thus avoiding a daunting two-way wartime train journey.

My long spell with Air Staff RAFNI came to an end with the culmination of a scheme hatched between Wing Commander John Cherry, Ops 2 at Fighter Command, and myself for a drastic reduction in the number of service personnel required to man the Control and Reporting organisation in Northern Ireland.

The plan was to put the last remaining sector operations room at Ballyhalbert on care and maintenance; and to concentrate the whole operation as a group/sector with its control room in the Senate Chamber at Stormont. Ballyhalbert would be left complete with all its communications as an emergency alternative should Stormont be destroyed.

During the switch over Northern Ireland would for several minutes be defenceless. As 'H' hour approached the Chief Signals Officer, Wg Cdr Gammack, Fg Off Ginn and F J De Courcy of the GPO were at my side, all brimming with confidence. At 11.00 am sharp the duty controller made his sign by dropping his handkerchief (high drama!). After about two minutes the signals officers reported that the job was done. "Test the Ballywooden GCI liaison line" I said. A moment later the sergeant duty controller looked up at the dias with a wicked grin on his face. "The American Forces Programme Strength Nine, Sir!"

As the result of this exercise air staff disappeared with the exception of the SASO. The rank of the AOC Northern Ireland was reduced to Air Commodore! Despite my somewhat Machiavellian part in the process, to my disappointment, I was retained stuck in Northern Ireland to combine C & R work done by myself as Air III with the position of Senior Controller of the new group/sector. The SASO Wing Commander John Butterworth was an easy intelligent man to get on with; and I had the consolation of promotion to Acting wing Commander. I hope the tax payer got some benefit from the manpower savings!

By this time the enemy were on the defensive although the Battle of the Atlantic was still raging with our convoys struggling home between the Mull of Kintyre and Rathlin Island, but there was no trade for our fighters with the lone exception of Findlay Boyd's encounter with his Condor away out beyond Malin Head.

CHAPTER 14
SENIOR CONTROLLER

RAF Northern Ireland proved an interesting staff appointment, but with insufficient action to keep the wheels of the control reporting organisation properly oiled. For that reason we were, I think, chosen as a place for training sector controllers who were who were now needed in much larger numbers to man GCI and other overseas Operations Rooms.

During my tenure as Senior Controller I was, therefore, employed by Fighter Command to run a course for Controllers under training - a thing I had been doing towards the end of my time at Prestwick. My students arrived quite suddenly at Ardtullagh without any warning to the mess secretary or his staff. When Colonel Dillon came down to breakfast all that remained on the table were a few overturned empty toast racks. "Locusts" exploded the hungry Colonel; and thus my students became known as "Mac's locusts."

My time as Senior Controller in Northern Ireland passed to its conclusion without any interruption from Hitler and Goering; but one incident is riveted in my memory. A Dutch Squadron at Ballyhalbert, equipped with Spitfires, were training to become operational by night. Their Commanding Officer was keen to fly, but I tried to put him off because the weather report was distinctly ominous. But off he went. Being uneasy in my mind after supper I went up to Stormont. No sooner had I arrived than Squadron Leader Tope, who was controlling, got a call on the RT from the Dutchman to say that his compass had failed. It must be the gyro compass I thought. I should explain that this was an instrument fitted to the Spitfire which enabled the pilot to fly the aircraft on to any course chosen by turning the fore and aft line of the aeroplane to coincide with the compass reading on what looked like a measuring tape right in the pilot's view. There was no need to bother with the pilot's compass which had given Pilot Officer Webb so much bother during his training.

"Tell him to try the pilot's compass" I said. "It's out of action too" replied Tope. That's incredible I thought; but there was no point in arguing. The storm clouds were getting lower and lower over the County Down coast. Tell him to orbit I said while we think. How about the moon, I thought, but where is it? "Ask him if he can see the moon?" "Yes he can". "Tell is the moon shining?" It must have been the first time someone had ever asked them that question, but within two minutes they had the answer. "From the east." Good enough. I dashed back to the Senate Chamber. "Tell him to keep the moon behind his right shoulder and come right down, he should break cloud at about 500 feet over the Irish coast" - and he did. The matter of the pilot's compass was never explained, but at least we had one live Dutchman.

About this time, by the courtesy of the staff of the Senior Naval Officer at Belfast Castle, I enjoyed a splendid day out as their guest on a corvette which was testing its mine throwers. In return I arranged to give the anti-aircraft gunners on one of their cruisers practice in aiming their guns. The fate of the Prince of Wales and the Repulse was still very much in my mind. The CO of the Polish Squadron at Ballyhalbert agreed to co-operate but, despite the careful arrangements made with the Navy at Belfast Castle, the cruiser ran to form and opened up with all its anti aircraft guns on the unfortunate Spitfire. I told the indignant Pole to stand clear while I got a message through to the Captain. I was duly reassured a few minutes later by Naval Headquarters at the Castle that all would be well – so round went the Pole once more. Immediately there was another indignant shout "They are shooting at me again, now I will go down and give them a burst". Oh my God what next! "Pancake at once" I cried. I never again attempted naval co-operation – which is a pity because we could have given them plenty of it.

1943 was a year of courses and conferences. To get a break from RAFNI, I volunteered for a Q planning course to be held in St James Street, London under American auspices. The accommodation and the food were marvellous; but Q planning was even duller than I expected. My role on the course was to answer any questions which might involve aeroplanes in the delivery of the vast array of items required by the army such as weapons and ammunition, food and petrol. Fortunately they had no need of my advice!

I was, however, much intrigued to hear about the experience we had gained from the preparations made for the invasion of North Africa. In order to load the ships for the "Torch" convoy the units taking part were called upon to detail their requirements and complete their bids for space in the ships. At this point things seem to have gone badly wrong. Commanding Officers of the units at the foot of the command cone would review the requirements of their quarter masters and then add 10% or even more for safety. Brigade would then add another 10% to be on the safe side, and so on upwards to Division and even higher, each adding in another percentage to their bid. According to the Q planners on our course the ships were stuffed full with so much cargo not needed for the initial invasion, that General Anderson could have landed a complete extra brigade.

Another mistake was just as bad, and could have produced a worse result if the enemy had been able to mount an air attack on the ships and the troops during the initial landings. According to our experts at St James Street the ships were crammed to capacity in a commercial manner which did not permit rapid tactical discharge of the essential cargo needed during the critical phase of the operation, during which the ships and their cargoes could have ben sent to the bottom of the Mediterranean Sea by a successful air attack.

Fortunately these lessons had been learned before our landing in Normandy on 6th June 1944.

During the autumn of 1943 I was sent on a course for Senior Commanders at RAF Cranwell where "bull" reigned supreme. I did not take to the place and the instructors did not take to me. They doubted whether I could quell a mutiny.

As John Butterworth, the SASO, was more or less chained to his desk I was lucky to be sent as the Command air staff representative to attend conferences in London and elsewhere. This gave me rather more scope for enjoyable flights round Britain in an Oxford.

On 13th May 1943 in Tunisia the enemy was finally cleared out of Africa. By the autumn American and British armies were fighting a bitter campaign in Italy resulting in the collapse of the Italians and the occupation of their country by the Nazis. The American forces in Britain were building up for the ultimate invasion of the Continent. The Germans were bogged down in Russia where the tide had turned. Ultimate victory was in sight. The threat of a German invasion of Eire had evaporated. In consequence Northern Ireland had become a holding base for American and British troops, but the Royal Navy and Coastal Command were still heavily engaged in the Battle of the Atlantic. Fighter Command with its extensive control and reporting system was inactive but had to be maintained at its full state of readiness. The Luftwaffe were heavily engaged on the Russian Front but still had large forces resting in France which could be used against us if they chose to step up the air war to the west. For our troops on the ground inactivity led to boredom. I had been appointed Senior Controller of the Group Sector in Northern Ireland at Stormont in the rank of Wing Commander, which I would gladly have relinquished to take part in the Second Front in a reduced rank – but not a hope – all the RAF control jobs were already bagged. My medical category was back at AIB so I could have tried for Bomber Command, but the show would probably be over before I could be ready for ops on heavy bombers.

Wing Commander Hector MacLean
BL, AE & Bar, DL
1948

probably be over before I could be ready for ops on heavy bombers.

One had but to hear the BBC reporting after each Bomber Command operation to realise the remarkable bravery of their crews. Our losses were averaging about three per cent of the aircraft engaged. Thirty raids were expected for the first tour of operations. Three times thirty being ninety it was indeed a tribute to the youth of Britain that the RAF never lacked a queue of volunteers for air crew.

About late 1943 those in charge of our fighter defences got themselves well and truly worked up about "window" - a new top secret Bomber Command device scarcely to be mentioned nor even discussed. It consisted of strips of paper coated with aluminium cut to match the wave lengths of the German defence radar. Aircraft in our attacking force would shower down this window over Germany in the path of the British raiders paralysing the enemy radar cover by producing an electric snowstorm on their screens.

Although Window was a brilliant concept it could so easily be turned against us once the enemy got the hang of it and began to cut their own foil to jam our defences. Meanwhile it was working well and our losses dropped as chaos reigned down below for the German controllers. But how long would it last before we were rumbled? As so often happens, there was an unseen problem. We had failed to warn the German cows! The poor beasts began to eat Window after which they became unwell and died. The German farmers grumbled and the cause of death was diagnosed.

I never heard what the enemy did about window, they may have changed their radar frequencies. Nor do I know whether they ever developed the system for raids on the United Kingdom. I doubt it because by that time their bombers were all needed in Russia, and on other active fronts. Moreover there was Hitler's secret weapon which he was preparing for London, and which would scarcely need radar protection.

In due course the V1 Flying Bombs arrived, soon to be followed by the V2 rockets.

Later in 1943 I was glad of a fortnight's course on combined operations at the Holywood Hotel, Largs. This proved an interesting and almost enjoyable experience for officers attending; but not quite such fun for those actually chosen and booked for D-Day in Normandy. At the conclusion of the course we were all asked for our comments on the plan which had been prepared by the Chief of Staff to the Allied Commander (COSAC) with his planning staff in London (without, of course, naming or hinting at the destination of the landings). My own expressed view was that there were insufficient infantry for the initial landings. Just before we dispersed Monty was appointed Commander in Chief of the combined land invasion forces, and was shown the COSAC plan. To my satisfaction his comment, couched in typical Montgomery language, was "Not enough forwards"!

In February 1945 I was posted to HQ 11 Group Uxbridge as one of the duty Group Controllers responsible for the air defences of London and the South-East of England. By this time we were advancing towards the Rhine. The German Air Force was battling for survival on two fronts with little time for raids on the United Kingdom. The Operations room was manned on a three watch basis which meant fifty-six hours a week of comparative boredom.

The menace of the V1 flying bomb and the V2 rockets (not openly discussed for security reasons) was waning as the allied ground forces pushed back the launching pads in Europe. This was just as well because there was nothing we at Ops could do about these weapons; although the anti-aircraft command had some success against the V1s. Our latest day fighters had just been able to catch the V1 flying bomb if they were lucky enough to intercept it from a dive. Some of our fighters were reported as flying alongside the bomb and with a wingtip under the bomb's wing easing it over to crash and blow up in open country. Thankfully the V2 rocket came just too late for the Germans because there was no answer to it

The conventional bomber strength of the Luftwaffe was fully occupied on both their fronts; but like all air forces they could be switched at short notice to a changed role. Hence the home air defence network had to be fully maintained to operate the night fighter and a reduced force of day fighter squadrons.

The main strength of our day fighters was now employed on the offensive fitted with long range disposable fuel tanks to give them the extra range for escorting the American day bomber raids over Germany. Fuel conservation was the vital factor and demanded exact timing for the rendezvous between fighters and the Americans. For the bombers or the fighters to be late or even early the casualties from enemy fighters could be horrendous. The planning for these escort operations was done down in the Group hole at Uxbridge by Wing Commander Keith Lofts and a Danish Lieutenant Colonel whose name I forget. For this they had a table map of Eastern Germany and the Low Countries over which the navigation experts had evolved and fitted a specially calibrated steel arm rather like an extended mounting for an angle poise lamp. The device incorporated a course speed calculator (CSC) which enabled the planner to take into account such matters as wind speed and direction needed to work out the timing, the air speed and the course our fighters were to fly.

I was particularly impressed by the brief clear orders issued to the squadrons by the planners shortly before take off. They were sent out by teleprinter on a pro forma style with separate paragraphs defining the Squadron's flight plan and exactly what each technical branch was to do. What I saw at 11 Group enabled me to tackle my last job in the war at Inverness where I was Wing Commander plans at 14 Group.

Although the Luftwaffe were almost finished by the beginning of March 1945, they had one freak card up their sleeve known as the "piggy back aircraft". This was a sea plane designed to carry a huge bomb. As it could not possibly take off armed with its heavy load the strike aircraft was mounted on the back of a large flying boat which could be flown towards the target to release it at flying speed and send it on its way. Presumably it would have needed a pilot to fly the sea plane and guide it to an appropriate target. To my knowledge the piggy back aircraft was never used and I sometimes wonder what might have happened to the unfortunate sea plane pilot after he had delivered his cargo. I suspect the enemy may have had some difficulty finding a willing volunteer! Be that as it may, on a day early in March 1945 Intelligence got a top secret message. The piggy back aircraft was coming that night. I was due on watch at 21.00 hours, but received a phone message from Jack Riddle to come down a quarter of an hour early. When I arrived the whole Ops Room was agog with expectation. To my disgust Jack handed me four sheets of paper densely typed on both sides. It was a special instruction from the AOC on how to destroy a piggy back aircraft with or without anti-aircraft guns and search lights, or by a combination of all three.

The raid was expected to come in somewhere between the Thames Estuary and Burnham on Crouch on the border of the 12 Group area. Complaining noises were already coming from the 12 Group Controller at Watnall. I got on to the Sector Controllers concerned to make sure that our night fighters went up in good time before darkness and went on reading that frightful instruction which was to be my bible in dealing with a situation which might only last for minutes, perhaps even seconds. One thing became clear; if 11Group intercepted, or if 12 Group got there first, we would all be heroes, and the darlings of the press; but if this speedy little sea plane slipped through in the darkness the AOC and Air Staff would be in the clear but the fall guy would be noneother than C H MacLean. At this point the AOC came on the line. "Had I read his instruction?" "Did I understand it?" "Yes Sir, and I am still studying it". "Do you know what to do?" The situation was difficult. He was known to be suffering from cancer. In a battle the enemy does not always do just what one expects him to do. I was being driven into a corner. "Yes, I think I do" was my reply, "But I'll have to deal with the situation in my discretion as it develops". My reply was not to his liking. Two days later I was posted to Middle Wallop as Senior Controller of the Sector, but to my surprise still in the rank of acting Wing Commander. Thankfully the piggy back aircraft never came. It is said of Queen Mary Tudor that when she died the word 'Calais' would be written on her heart. At least 'piggy back' will not be found written on mine!

To my delight as Senior Controller at RAF Station Middle Wallop I came under none other but Wing Commander John Dunlop Urie as Sector Commander. He had just been returned as time expired from his tour in the Middle East where his AOC had been so impressed with his staff work that he had, without his knowledge, put him up for a permanent commission. In the meantime he had (against my advice) decided to become a lawyer so when the formal offer came through he declined it. At that point I made a note to recruit him as a partner for our firm when he was qualified.

The Operations personnel and Dunlop's office were housed in Nether Wallop House with my Sector Operations Room at Over Wallop a few miles up the little river busily growing its watercress for the London restaurants. For contact with the squadrons, which were based at better tactical 11 Group locations, we had an Oxford and an Auster. These we flew from Middle Wallop aerodrome, by then a Royal Navy air station, under the command of Captain ("Blood") Ede, a distinguished sailor and a born Station Commander. Our officers were accommodated on the station and we shared their ward room.

Our sector pilot was none other than Flight Lieutenant R Muspratt-Williams. I soon got Sprat cracking in our Oxford flying as a target for sector interception exercises. The war was nearly over so something had to be done to keep the troops occupied.

The war in the Pacific was still in full swing with our forces leaping from island to island on their way to Japan. At each stage fighters and fighter control rooms were needed to protect their progress against air attack. It was to be the task of our senior service to provide Mobile Naval Operations Air Bases (MONABS). The mobile vehicles were assembled at Royal Naval Air Station, Middle Wallop, and the personnel trained to operate them. When operational the complete MONAB would be shipped out to the Pacific theatre.

Commander Keen Miller, the Commander flying at Middle Wallop was equipped with t Spitfire Mk.IX which he allowed me to fly. It proved a magnificent aeroplane and a considerable improvement on the Mk.I which we flew when the war began.

My next brush with the Reaper happened while flying the Auster from Middle Wallop. This aircraft was fitted for dual control with two separate joy sticks connected laterally by a stout aluminium bar down below knee level. The wind was blowing at about 50 to 60 miles an hour which required a steep gliding angle with plenty of air speed coming into land. The moment had come to flatten out so I pulled back on the control column. To my horror it was frozen solid. "My God" I thought, "I am going to be killed in this bloody Auster". Immediately I glanced down and there was the connecting bar jammed against the aluminium casing of my artificial leg. I pulled my leg clear and backed with the stick just in time to land with not more than a second to spare. Another life used up!

I lay awake that night wondering what sort of conclusion the fatal crash enquiry would have reached on the evidence. "Rusty Staff Officer failed to cope with a new type". Whatever the verdict it would have been pilot error which it certainly might have been, but it makes me wonder how often flying disasters officially described in a bland way as 'pilot error' may have been caused by some little detail or mishap no one could possibly have thought of. Not much later there was to be another similar incident.

The war in Europe had dragged to its conclusion with the suicide of Hitler and the surrender of the German Forces on 8th May 1945. There was much rejoicing in Britain but no joy for the Poles for whose freedom we had declared war in September 1939. After all their suffering they were back to square one under a sinister communist dictator. Understandably there were sour looks from some of our Polish friends in the RAF; but there was little we could do about it short of a military clash with the Russians, which was out of the question. Indeed the British people were clearly fed up with war and made this abundantly clear in the General Election by which the Government and our great war leader were dismissed from office on 26th July 1945.

Although the operational role of the Control and Reporting System had come to a sudden end in our theatre of the war on 8th May 1945, the organisation provided a magnificent reserve of trained personnel and technical equipment to support our fighters as and when they would be sent to the Far East. At the time we knew nothing of the atom bomb so it was essential to maintain the fighter squadrons, the GCIs and the radar crews at fully operational standards. I, therefore, stepped up our training with more live interception exercises. These were popular with the boys; but many of the operations room personnel were more interested in going home! However, I managed to explain the matter, and on the whole they took it well giving me their full co-operation, but I could see problems ahead. "I couldn't care less" was a phrase which was creeping into telephone conversations. I forbade this expression in our operations room at Over Wallop - as I still do to this day!

Just about this time the RAF began returning to civil life personnel qualified for release by age and length of service, Each of these lucky people were to be interviewed by an officer and told that they were not being discharged from the service but just released from duty. My first interview did not go well with an elderly WAAF from the cook house. "You are not being discharged from the RAF but released from your duties" I told her. Her eager face fell. "What does that mean, Sir"? "Well I suppose they might just want you again" I replied. "Why?" she insisted. "I'm sorry" I said, "they didn't tell me that, I was just told to explain the matter as I have done." But she was very persistent. "Can't you just tell me the reason." At this point I went off the rails. "Well," I said, "the Japs are not beaten yet, and we are having trouble with the Russians about Europe. The war was all about freedom. I suppose they think you might be needed again, but I doubt it". She threw up her arms and rgarded me in horror; but to my relief she eventually signed the form on the dotted line. It would have been awkward if she had refused to do so because there were no instructions on how to deal with that possibility!

In the meantime our Forces in the Far East were still locked in battle against an implacable enemy who could not even dream of surrender, with every one of their men expected, and apparently willing, to die at his post, or even commit suicide before yielding an inch of Japanese soil. Winston Churchill records in his book a military estimate that to conquer Japan yard by yard it might cost a million American and half a million British lives,;and that in addition to the Japanese losses.

The future for our troops in the Far Eastern theatre of operations was grim indeed; and not least for my brother, Major Bruce MacLean, Adjutant of the Second Battalion of the Black Watch, which had just been retrained as a parachute regiment to take part in an invasion to drive the Japanese out of Malaya where they would, in the jungle, be up against an enemy who looked not unlike the local population. Fortunately for the Black Watch, and unfortunately for the people of Hiroshima, on the 6th and the people of Nagasaki on the 9th of August 1945, the Malayan operation was never mounted, because the Japanese had surrendered. Faced with this ghastly new weapon there was at least a face saver and perhaps an honourable excuse for the Japanese High Command to advise the Emperor to capitulate. In retrospect our gratitude is due to the people of these two unfortunate cities. As a result of their sacrifice strategic theory instantly became strategic hard fact. It was a fact that has obviated major war for the remainder of the Twentieth Century and could well do so until the human race learns a better way of settling its disputes.

By mid-August the Fighter Defence organisation was running down, and I was once more on the move.

From Middle Wallop I was posted to HQ 14 Group at Drumossie, just south of Inverness. As the war was nearly over there was not much work left for me as Wing Commander on the staff responsible for planning, except for the organisation of a few large scale exercises. However, the work provided an opportunity of flying by Proctor or by Oxford to various establishments under our command which enabled me to visit places such as Stornoway and Orkney.

On a return flight from Turnhouse to Longmans airfield Inverness I agreed to take on board a young WAAF officer as passenger. With the girl strapped into the co-pilots seat in the Oxford off we flew to Inverness. The clouds were between four and five thousand feet at ten tenths giving clearance over the Cairngorms and other mountains en route. With RT available it seemed a good opportunity to brush up on my instrument flying so I spent most of the time in cloud, flying on the instruments with the Oxford nicely trimmed and with my fingers just touching the stick. Suddenly it was wrenched out of my hand and the Oxford zoomed upwards out of control. Looking round I saw the cause. The wretched WAAF, feeling uncomfortable under her straps, was using the co-pilots control column as a hand hold to lever her bottom to a better position on the seat. After a number of horrible contortions I got the aeroplane more or less under control emerging below the clouds in a dive with a few hundred feet to spare right over the top of Cairngorm itself. That was my last brush with the Reaper.

Before my release I flew a Proctor from Longmans to Abbotsinch with yet another WAAF sitting beside me as a passenger. The view was marvellous with the majestic Cairngorms to port and the formidable Nevis Group far on the starboard side. I was on top of the world; but as we cleared the Monadhliath Mountains over Newtonmore we hit a shocking bump and my passenger discharged her breakfast, most of which I managed to field with my nice new map. The rest of the flight was not quite so pleasant!

I was released from the RAF on 3rd September 1945 at Wembley where they presented me with a raincoat, a pair of trousers and a jacket together with a cheque for £150, if I remember correctly.

Flush with my gratuity and wearing my new raincoat I went home, took some leave and resumed my employment as a clerk; but soon to be a partner in the legal firm of Montgomerie, Flemings, Fyfe, MacLean and Co in Glasgow

In the meantime the Royal Air Force were rapidly releasing all but a few of the men and women who had been manning the Command, Group and Sector Operations rooms, the GCI stations and the coastal radar chain installations. At the height of the war there had, I believe, been nearly 50,000 (mostly women) employed on this work.

Although all kinds of new highly sophisticated secret radar developments for the detection of raids and the control of fighters were in the course of development, the RAF still had to rely on the existing control rooms and radar installations to provide fighter cover in the event of a further national emergency; which would, of course, need an immediate influx from civil life of released personnel with the necessary training.

As matters stood all the remaining regular officers, airmen and WAAFS of the C & R branch were needed to keep the system and the installations in working condition. This was moreover an essential element for keeping the remaining fighter squadrons operational, but no way could they have functioned by themselves in war time conditions without far more trained manpower.

The answer came in 1947 by raising the Fighter Control Units (FCUs) in the newly named Royal Auxiliary Air Force (RAuxAF).

These FCUs were established in the proximity of large towns and centres of population, and whenever possible near an existing Fighter Control complex. If I remember correctly 3603, the Edinburgh FCU, was fortunate in this respect the command of 3602 FCU and recommissioned (in the rank of Wing Commander).

Glasgow's FCU was based in the rather uninspiring RAF depot at Bishopbriggs which had no adjacent control installations; so we went to work building a dummy operations room which was soon up and running.

The role of the FCU. was to train men and women to man the operations rooms and other C & R functions of the RAF in the event of war. At Bishopbriggs we soon had plenty of young auxiliary volunteers, also a handful of regulars and a small cadre of auxiliary veterans. I was lucky to have a small group of auxiliary officers with wartime experience including the everlasting Tiny Gemmill RFC, RAF, as my second in command.

After my remarriage in June 1949 I handed over 3602 to Flight Lieutenant B S (Barney) Sandeman who had been acting Group Captain in the war. He in turn was succeeded by Wing Commander Bill Walker. By this time the C & R system, as we knew it, was undergoing a technical metamorphosis which greatly reduced the required manpower, and needed a higher degree of special training and ability for which regular personnel were more suited.

Our thanks are due to all the men and women who gave their time voluntarily to this work on behalf of Britain, and Glasgow in particular, whose people were able to get on with their lives while some provision was being made against outbreak of further hostilities and surprise air attack during the nine year life of the Fighter Control Units, during which the Cold War began to develop.

CHAPTER 15
IN MEMORIAM

In writing briefly about some of those who did not survive the Second World War I am deeply conscious that the losses 602 suffered in the offensive phase of its operations which began in 1941 are not mentioned. The Squadronís fighter sweeps over France and the Low Countries, and its support of our ground forces after the invasion of Europe, resulted in more casualties than those we suffered in the first defensive phase of the war. Two of our Squadron Commanders, Paddy Finucane DSO, DFC, and Chris Le Roux DFC, lost their lives in these operations. As I had lost all touch with 602 it is not for me to try to describe their part in the war after April 1941. All one can do is to take off one's hat in memory of those who flew and did not return.

What follows are some notes about some of those who served in the first defensive phase of the Squadrons operations who gave their lives during the war in a just cause. In citing the following names and brief particulars I have relied heavily on "Men of the Battle of Britain" by Kenneth G Wynn.

SERGEANT BRACKTON
No details known. Could have survived.

SERGEANT BRYDON
Trained at RAFVR Prestwick. Came to the Squadron on mobilisation on 24th August 1939. Crashed on practice night flight take off about 30th August 1939, and was killed.

70142 WILLIAM HUGH COVERLEY
Son of Thomas Craven Coverley killed at Cambrae in 1917.
On 7th July 1940 he shared in the destruction of a Ju88 but was shot down by enemy fighters near Dorchester and baled out. On 7th September he was shot down again and baled out. His aircraft crashed at Fosters Farm near Tonbridge. His body was later found caught up in a tree.

46566 FLYING OFFICER ALLEN LAIRD EDY, DFC

From Winnipeg, Canada. Volunteered and joined 602 Squadron at Westhampnett on 8th September 1940. He claimed a Dornier 17 destroyed on the 15th. Posted to 613 Squadron and was awarded the DFC on 5th November 1940. He was killed with 457 Squadron on 12th December 1941 and is buried at St Andrews Churchyard, Andrias, Isle of Man.

740713 SERGRANT DOUGLAS WILLIAM ELCOME

Trained in the RAFVR and 14 FTS. Joined 602 early in June 1940. Claimed a Bf109 destroyed over Dungeness on 31st August 1940. On 10th September he crashed on Felpham Golf Course during flying practice. On 20th October Elcome failed to return from patrol. Reported missing. He is remembered in the Runnymede Memorial Panel 14.

PILOT OFFICER DOUGLAS HUGH GAGE

Shrewsbury School 1931 - 1935. Joined 602 at Westhampnet on 21 September 1940. Jumped on the 27th and force-landed Mayfield. 30 October surprise attack by Me 109 - force-landed at Hornchurch. Killed 6 June 1941 when with 32 squadron at Hawkinge. Runnymede Memorial Panel 32.

473117 FLIGHT LIEUTENANT JAMES GILLIES, MC, DFM

Joined the Squadron on 18th September 1940. Claimed shared destruction of a Ju88 on the 21st September and claimed a Me110 on 26th September. Served in 421 Flight then 91 Squadron. On 11th January 1941 destroyed a float plane and an Me109 and another on 18th September. Awarded DFM on 30th May 1941. Commissioned November 1941. Killed on 24th April 1944 with 135 Squadron, aged 29. Gazetted for the MC on 13th February 1945 in respect of an arms dump operation. Remembered on Singapore Memorial column 431.

FLYING OFFICER NIGEL GRAEME

He came to 602 from 607 Squadron and flew with B Flight. He returned to 607 before the war and was, I believe, killed in a Hurricane before the evacuation of Dunkirk.

81357 SQUADRON LEADER OSGOOD VILLIERS HANBURY (Pedro), DSO, DFC & Bar

Joined 602 during August 1940. He claimed to have destroyed a Do17 on 15th September.

On 21st September he shared a Ju88. He claimed a Ju88 on 30th September and a Bf109 on 30th October. He joined 260 Squadron and destroyed a Ju88 in the desert on 14th December 1941. In March 1942 he was given command of the Squadron and shared a Bf109. On 3rd April he destroyed a Ju87 and a MC202. On the 25th he was himself hit and force landed near Gazala. He was awarded the DFC on 22nd May 1942 and then destroyed a Bf109 and probably another on 27th June. He was given a Bar to his DFC on 28th July 1942. Hanbury resumed command of 260 Squadron on 2nd November 1942. He then claimed a Bf109 destroyed on 2nd January 1943 and a Bf110 on 17th April. He was awarded the DSO on 30 April 1943. I only knew Pedro for a few days but agree with Donald Jack's description of him as a man of great charm and a dedicated pilot who became a great leader and who never let his success in the Western Desert go to his head, which is just what one would expect from an 'Old Etonian'. Hanbury is reported to have been killed flying with 117 Squadron, but it was also rumoured that he died with some other pilots in the Hudson returning to Britain in which Leslie Howard, the film star, lost his life, shot down in the Bay of Biscay. He is remembered in the Runnymede Memorial Panel 118.

81047 PILOT OFFICER ARCHIBALD LYALL

He was the son of an HLI Officer killed in action in France in July 1916.
Pat Lyall joined the Squadron in March 1940 as a Sergeant Pilot and was commissioned in April 1940. On 9th September he claimed a Bf109 and a Do17 destroyed and another Do 17 on the 15th. On the 21st September he shared a Ju88 and on 29th October a Bf 109 and on 6th November probably another Bf109. Lyall was shot down over the Isle of Wight on 28th November 1940. He baled out too low and was killed in his 28th year. His remains were cremated at Woodvale, Brighton.

90168 SQUADRON LEADER ARCHIBALD ASHMORE McKELLAR, DSO, DFC & BAR.

Archie shared with George Pinkerton in shooting down a He111 on 28th October 1939. It crashed at Kidlaw being the first enemy aircraft to fall on British soil. He was posted to 605 County of Warwick Squadron on 21st June 1940 as a Flight Commander. On 15th August he claimed three He111s in defence of Newcastle-upon-Tyne. On 9th September he destroyed three He111s and a Me109. On the 11th he shared a He111. On 15th he shot down two more Me109s and a Do17, and on the 16th an He111.

On 29th September Archie took command of 605 Squadron and on 7th October claimed 5 Me 109s destroyed; and then between the 20th, the 26th and the 27th three more Me 109s.

Archie was shot down and killed on 1st November 1940. His Hurricane crashed at Woodlands Addisham. He was awarded the DFC on 13th September 1940, a Bar to the DFC on 8th October 1940 and the DSO on 26th November 1940. He is buried at Eastwood Cemetary.

81046 PILOT OFFICER HENRY WALLASTON MOODY Aged 30.
Joined 602 in March 1940 as Sergeant Pilot. Harry was commissioned in April 1940. He broke his collar bone when he slipped climbing into a Spitfire.

On 18th August Moody claimed a Ju87 destroyed. The next day his aircraft was set ablaze by return fire from a Ju88 over Bognor. He baled out and landed in the precincts of a girl's school. Moody claimed a Dornier 17 on 4th September but failed to return from combat over the Biggin Hill area three days later and was reported missing. He is remembered on the Runnymede Memorial panel 9.

PILOT OFFICER ROY AINLEY PAYNE
Joined 602 on 3 September 1940 from an Army Co-operation squadron. Killed later in the war.

741471 SERGEANT JACK PROCTOR
Came from Coventry. Sergeant joined 602 at Drem on 21st June 1940. He claimed a Ju88 destroyed on 31st August 1940, a Bf109 on 6th September, a Bf110 on the 7th and another on the 11th. Jack Proctor was killed on 18th April 1941 aged 24 and is buried in Coventry.

73010 FLYING OFFICER THOMAS GLYN FINLAYSON RITCHIE
Glyn was commissioned in the RAFVR in March 1939 and joined 602 Squadron on mobilisation. On 19th August 1940 Ritchie shared in the destruction of a Ju88. On the 23rd September he successfully returned to Westhampnett after colliding in a cloud with another RAF fighter. He claimed a Bf110 destroyed on the 25th September but was wounded in the legs over Hailsham on the 26th and admitted to hospital. By 1941 Glyn was in command of

A Flight. On 21st July the Squadron escorted three Stirlings to attack a target at Lille. On the way they were jumped by Bf109s. Ritchie was shot down and killed. He was greatly missed by all his friends, his death was not only a loss to the Squadron but to the City of Glasgow where he had a bright future before him. Glyn is buried in Reninghelst Churchyard extension, Belgium.

741141 SERGEANT MERVYN HERBERT SPRAGUE

Born 27th May 1910. Sprague served in the RAF Reserve from 1935 to 1938. On 18th June 1940 he joined 602 at Drem. Sprague was shot down by enemy fighters on 25th August but baled out. He was rescued unhurt from the sea but on 11th September he was shot down again and killed in combat with a Messerschmitt 110 south of Selsey Bill. His body was washed up at Brighton on 10th October. He is buried at Tangmere. Sadly his fiancÈe could not believe it and for many days sat in a motor car at the end of the airfield waiting for his return.

740484 SERGEANT BASIL EWART PATRICK WHALL

Joined RAFVR in 1936. After mobilisation he joined 605 Squadron at Tangmere and 263 Squadron in April 1940. On 21st April the Squadron embarked on HMS Furious and landed on a frozen fjord in Norway. By 26th April all their Gladiators were either unserviceable or destroyed so the Squadron re-embarked for the United Kingdom. They went back again in May. Between 21st May and 6th June Whall destroyed a Dornier 17 and two more German aircraft before the enemy bombed the ice and the personnel were withdrawn. He was fortunate to survive the sinking of the Glorious, and was awarded the DFM for his efforts. Whall came to 602 at Drem on 5th July 1940. He shared a Dornier 17 on 15th August and destroyed two Ju87s on the 18th. In this engagement his Spitfire L1019 was hit by return fire and he ditched at Elmer Sands, Middleton writing off the aircraft. On 26th August Whall claimed two Heinkel 110s destroyed. On 7th September a 109 and on the 9th a Dornier 17. Then on the 30th he shared a Ju88 and on 7th October shared a probable Dornier 17. On this day his Spitfire X4160 may have been damaged by a Ju88 off Beachy Head. To the surprise of Donald Jack, his leader, on the way back Whall's aircraft suddenly went down and crashed while he was attempting a forced landing. He was taken to Princess Alice Hospital, Eastbourne, severely injured and died on admission. There was something rather mysterious about the way Whall crashed. There was a whiff of sabotage about it, which was never cleared up. Aged 22 at the time of his death he was already an ace pilot and had all the makings of a star turn. Without doubt he would soon have been commissioned. He is buried at St Marys Churchyard, Amersham in Buckinghamshire.

741028 SERGEANT GEORGE ALBERT WHIPPS

Joined 602 at Drem on 21st June 1940. He was shot down in combat with BF109s over Hailsham on 6th September but baled out unhurt. On 29th October he claimed a BF109 destroyed. In August 1941 Whipps was a Flight Sergeant Instructor at 61 OTU at Heston. He was with a pupil in a Miles Master trainer. They were both killed when a Belgian pilot in a Spitfire did not check the runway was clear and took the hood off the Master. The Belgian himself was killed in similar circumstances on 6th November when a Spitfire landed on top of his taxiing aircraft. Whipps is buried at St Marys Churchyard, Theydon Bois, Essex.

ADDENDUM
WINGS OVER THE SEA

The first overseas flight by the Royal Flying Corps was achieved by my uncle; Captain Archibald Campbell Holms MacLean in a BE2 dual controlled aeroplane No 272 in September 1913. It may be of interest to hear how this came about.

In 1912 as a young Lieutenant in the Royal Scots with the ability to see beyond the end of his nose, Campbell MacLean spotted the significance of the aeroplane for military operations. He saw that it offered prospects beyond the expectation of an infantry officer. The RFC seemed willing enough to have him seconded from the Royal Scots, but not until he had learned fly. He would have to pay for this himself; so my grandfather Charles James MacLean would have to fork out. Needless to say my grandparents were less than enthusiastic. "That's a damned dangerous thing to get involved in, Campbell" was the comment of my father, his elder brother. "Not a bit" replied my uncle, "if there's a war I will be so high up I will be out of harms way". That settled it, and his father paid up. Curiously enough and, no doubt to his disappointment, Campbell's prediction proved correct. In 1915 when he took command of a squadron in France he was under orders not to fly. At that point the RFC were short of senior officers with experience in this new branch of the service and were not prepared to lose them in combat.

Campbell MacLean soon went solo and was seconded to the RFC in the autumn of 1912 when he joined No 4 Squadron flying Maurice Farmans and Breguets. He was keen to fly the BE2 and so in the spring of 1913 managed to get himself posted to No 2 Squadron who were equipped with this advanced aeroplane.

Campbell must have mastered the BE2 because in September 1913 he was promoted Captain and selected to fly a BE2 to Ireland to attend and take part in the annual army manoeuvres.

According to my grandmother, the first stage of the flight took my uncle to Galloway where he landed in a large field on the estate of Lord Stair. At this stage he intended to fill up with petrol to get himself safely across the St George's Channel from Portpatrick to Northern Ireland, and thence to the manoeuvres in County Limerick. He was gladly received by his Lordship and I believe spent the night as his guest. Before leaving, Stair invited the

Captain to view his private museum. To the horror of my uncle one of the prize artefacts in the museum was a BE2 propeller which could only have come from one source! If it remained - the flight was over! It must have been an embarrassing anticlimax to the visit when this novel exhibit was removed from the museum and rebolted on to the aeroplane.

Presumably the remainder of the flight went to plan; but on his return flight, judging from the report published in the Ayrshire Post on 3rd October 1913, the pilot appears either to have been blown off course or made use of a south-westerly tail wind to advance further on his journey up the Ayrshire coast. The report read as follows:

"Shortly after 1.00 p.m. on Friday 26th September 1913 a lone bi-plane passed over the town of Ayr heading north. This event caused some interest as it was the first aeroplane ever to be seen by many of the town's people. The aircraft, a BE2, serial number 272 belonging to No 2 Squadron Royal Flying Corps, continued to Troon where it landed on the golf course near Southwood. The pilot, Captain MacLean, was on route in a series of short hops from army manoeuvres at Rathbone Camp in County Limerick to his base at Panmure Barracks, Montrose. He had departed from Newcastle, County Down, intending to land at Coults Farm near Castle Kennedy in Galloway, but due to bad weather had strayed many miles off course. He chanced upon the open smooth fairways of the golf course at Troon where he set his aircraft

Captain A C H MacLean

down safely. On the following morning he took off to resume his journey but was forced to land again almost immediately because of the haze. Captain MacLean stayed the weekend in Troon as the guest of Mr Richard Allen of Dunalton. He left on Monday 29th September and was after some exciting adventures in East Dunbartonshire and again in the neighbourhood of Coupar, he arrived safely at Montrose."

Mr Hood of Troon who took the trouble to research the flight comments as follows:

"Could MacLean have been the first pilot ever to take advantage of the 'window' of clear weather between Troon and Ayr? This weather phenomenon became well known to the early commercial aviators and largely because of it an aerodrome was later established near Monkton. Over the years this airfield grew and became Prestwick Airport which is still noted for its excellent weather record."

Captain Longcroft regarded as the star pilot of No 2 Squadron won the Britannia Trophy for 1913 by flying non-stop from Montrose to Farnborough on 22nd November in a modified BE2. This was, on that day a world record, and his name was inserted in the FII record book. Unfortunately an Italian flew slightly further a few days later and Longcroftís name was scratched out of the record book in favour of this pilot.

In the meantime A C H MacLean was appointed Landings Officer for his Squadron. This entailed travelling round Britain by air and in a vintage motor car looking over hedges and choosing aerodromes; an activity not covered by his studies at Kelvinside and Sandhurst! My mother accompanied him on some of these sorties including one towards the flat land between Paisley and the Clyde. On looking over a hedge at Renfrew behold there was an aeroplane attended by a group of enthusiasts under the leadership of a Mr Weir, of Cathcart fame. They hurried in and made themselves known. After a brief inspection Campbell concluded that if Weir could do it then the place ought to suit the RFC; and that is how Renfrew aerodrome came about. There were many other similar selections; but sadly with the casual indifference of youth I never asked my uncle for a list. He was definite about Renfrew and Church Fenton. Loch Doon was selected against his advice and failed. I think he mentioned Turnhouse and a place on the Ayrshire coast. Possibly it was Gailes.

It is interesting to note that the standard test to find if a field it was suitable for flying at that time was to drive over it at thirty miles an hour. If the car survived the test had been passed!

In December 1913 Captain MacLean was appointed as a Flying Instructor at the Central Flying School (CFS). He finished there as Chief Flying Instructor (CFI) after which he joined No 1 Squadron forming at Brooklands. In October 1914 he took over command of No 5 Squadron in France replacing the Commanding Officer who had been wounded.

In May 1915 Major MacLean was sent home sick, but after three months he returned to

France to command No 8 Squadron.

A year later my uncle was promoted to Lt Colonel in command of No 8 Wing at Catterick with a role of training pilots to strafe Zeppelins and to form new Squadrons.

In August 1916 he was appointed Commandant of CFS.

In November 1917 he took command of RAF Uxbridge which was built during the period of his appointment. From Uxbridge in 1918 he was promoted Acting Brigadier General and posted to the South East area a Chief Staff Officer. His last appointment in 1918 was to RAF Cologne.

According to my Grandmother General Trenchard asked my uncle how things were going in Germany, but was not too pleased when General MacLean told him there was not enough to do. In the autumn of 1919 the blow fell. The RAF was shrinking to its peace time establishment. It must have been a bitter pill for Campbell MacLean to swallow when he found himself back at Glencorse barracks near Edinburgh in command of the Royal Scots depot in his substantive army rank of Major.

I only met Lord Dowding once as a Battle of Britain Pilots' Reunion. I had the temerity to ask him if had known my uncle and whether he had ever received any flying instruction from him. "No" he said "I had to pay for that myself, but I will tell you a good story about your uncle". When he was Commandant of the CFS in 1916 he was driven to distraction by the frustration of communicating with his pupils by speaking tubes. One day he lined up six pupils and gave them this order. "Follow me. Everything I do you do". So off they went. The Commandant looped and spun and he rolled followed by his faithful pupils. All went well until Campbell's engine failed and he force landed. Out he climbed with that sense of satisfaction one gets after a successful forced landing, but suddenly he observed six aeroplanes approaching in line astern. With horror he recalled his order "Everything I do you do". Despite his frantic gestures inexorably in they came and upside down they all went.

Early in 1940 Pilot Officer A C H MacLean RAFVR was reaccepted into the RAF. On reporting for duty he was interviewed by his AOC who turned out to be one of his war time pupils to whom he had, indeed, presented with his Wings. He soon found himself as Acting Wing Commander in the personnel branch at 11 Group.

It may surprise some readers of the modern generation to learn that the Japanese were our allies in the Great War. I have never been clear about what they did, but they certainly made a shrewd decision by sending a group of young Japanese officers to the RFC for pilot training at the Central Flying School under the supervision of the Commandant, Colonel A C

H MacLean, who was duly rewarded by their Emperor with the Order of the Rising Sun Second Class. This splendid looking ribbon had to be removed from my uncle's tunic in 1942 when the Japanese joined the band wagon with Hitter and Mussolini. Not only had Japan become our enemy, but the medal may well have been a reward for training some of the air officers responsible for the incredibly successful attack on Pearl Harbour. "The best laid plans of mice and men oft gang a'glay".

After the Battle of Britain Campbell MacLean was sent to Canada to help in the formation of the Royal Canadian Air Force (RCAF) in which he ended up as Director of Personnel at their headquarters until the autumn of 1942. Thereafter he was promoted Group Captain Air Liaison Officer with the London Area until the end of the war in 1945 when he reverted to his army rank of full Colonel and was awarded the CBE.

Appendix I

No. 602 (City of Glasgow) Squadron
Commanding Officers

Sqn Ldr C N Lowe MC DFC	Sept 1925 – Jan 1926
Capt J D Latta MC (First Auxiliary CO)	Feb 1926 – May 1927
Sqn Ldr J Fullerton	May 1927 – May 1932
Sqn Ldr, The Marquess of Douglas and Clydesdale AFC	May 1932 – Sept 1936
Sqn Ldr D F McIntyre AFC	Sept 1936 – Oct 1937
Sqn Ldr A D Farquhar DFC	Oct 1937 – Apr 1940
Sqn Ldr G C Pinkerton OBE DFC	Apr 1940 – July 1940
Sqn Ldr A V R (Sandy) Johnstone DFC	Jul 1940 – Apr 1941
Sqn Ldr J I Kilmartin OBE DFC	Apr 1941 – Jun 1941
Sqn Ldr P Meagher	Jun 1941 – Aug 1941
Sqn Ldr A C (Al) Deere DSO OBE DFC	Aug 1941 – Jan 1942
Sqn Ldr B (Paddy) Finucane DSO DFC (Killed in action 1944)	Jan 1942 – Oct 1942
Sqn Ldr P M Brothers DSO DFC	Jun 1942 – Oct 1942
Sqn Ldr M F Beytagh DFC	Oct 1942 – Oct 1943
Sqn Ldr R A (Max) Sutherland DFC	Oct 1943 – Jul 1944
Sqn Ldr J J (Chris) Le Roux DFC (Killed in action)	Jul 1944 – Aug 1944
Sqn Ldr R A (Max) Sutherland DFC	Aug 1944 – May 1945
Sqn Ldr M Robinson AFC (Reformed 602 after the war)	Sep 1946 – Aug 1950
Sqn Ldr H M Stephen DSO DFC	Sep 1950 – Jul 1952
Sqn Ldr J A (Jack) Forrest (Joined 602 as NCO pilot - last Aux CO)	Jul 1952 – Oct 1953
Sqn Ldr R B (Bert) Davidson DFC	Oct 1953 – May 1956
Sqn Ldr C D (Don) Bartman	May 1956 – Mar 1957

Appendix II

Officers and aircrew at the outbreak of War
3 September 1939
(In order of seriority)

Sqn Ldr A D Farquhar – Officer Commanding
Flt Lt G C Pinkerton – OC 'B' Flight
Flt Lt M Robinson – OC 'A' Flight
Flt Lt E V N Bell (Auxiliary Adjutant)
Fg Off J H Hodge (AAF Reserve)
Fg Off A M Grant (AAF Reserve)
Fg Off A V R Johnstone
Fg Off J D Urie
Fg Off R Muspratt-Williams
Fg Off R F Boyd
Fg Off C H MacLean
Fg Off P J Ferguson
Fg Off A A McKellar
Fg Off D M Jack
Fg Off P E Webb
Plt Off N Graeme
Fg Off N Stone
Plt Off H G Niven
Plt Off T G Ritchie
Sgt R F Philips
Sgt A McDowall
Sgt J M Bryden
Sgt D W Macadam
Sqn Ldr J C W Allan (Medical Officer)
Rev Lewis A Sutherland (Padre - Minister of the Holy Rude Church, Stirling)

Appendix III

Officers and aircrew during the Battle of Britain
July 1940 – September 1940

Squadron Leader A V R Johnstone - Officer Commanding

Flt Lt J D Urie (OC 'A' Flt)	Plt Off H W Moody (Killed during Battle)
Flt Lt R F Boyd (OC 'B' Flt)	Plt Off H G Niven
Fg Off P C C Barthropp	Plt Off R A Payne (later killed in action)
Fg Off W H Coverley (Killed during Battle)	Plt Off T G F Ritchie (later killed in action)
Fg Off P J Ferguson	Plt Off S N Rose
Fg Off J S Hart	Flt Sgt J Gillies (Killed during Battle)
Fg Off C H MacLean (OC 'A' Flt after Urie)	Sgt C F Babbage
Fg Off C J Mount (OC 'A' Flt after MacLean)	Sgt Bracton
Fg Off P C Webb	Sgt A W Eade
Plt Off E W Aries	Sgt D W Elcombe (Killed during Battle)
Plt Off A L Edy (later killed in action)	Sgt A McDowall
Plt Off G Fisher	Sgt J Proctor
Plt Off D H Gage (later killed in action)	Sgt L S Smith
Plt Off O V Hanbury (later killed in action)	Sgt W B Smith
Plt Off W P Hopkin	Sgt W M Sprague (Killed during Battle)
Plt Off D M Jack	Sgt B E P Whall (Killed during Battle)
Plt Off A Lyall (later killed in action)	Sgt G A Whipps (later killed in flying accident)

Appendix IV
Index of people mentioned
Ranks stated are probably those held at the completion of service
(apologies for any omissions or inaccuracies).

Appendix V
Index of airfields, establishments and places

Appendix VI
Index of aircraft and squadrons

* Aircraft flown by the Author

Appendix VII
The 602 Squadron Museum Association

The 602 Squadron Museum was officially opened on 22 October 1983 by Marshal of the Royal Air Force, The Lord Cameron of Balhousie. It was built to commemorate the outstanding achievements of No.602 (City of Glasgow) Squadron, Royal Auxiliary Air Force from its formation in 1925 until its disbandment in 1957.

602 was the first of 21 auxiliary squadrons to be formed within the Royal Air Force and began flying from Moorpark aerodrome at Renfrew. It was originally a bomber squadron but converted to fighters in May 1939. Two of its pilots, The Marquis of Douglas & Clydesdale (later the Duke of Hamilton) and Flight Lieutenant David McIntyre, were the first men ever to fly over Mount Everest. Such was the confidence of the Air Ministry in this unit that 602 was the first Auxiliary Squadron to be equipped with Spitfires - and, indeed, 7th in the whole Royal Air Force. With these Spitfires it was involved in the shooting down of the first German aircraft in UK skies in the Second World War. Later, the Squadron moved south into the thick of the Battle of Britain where it soon established itself as one of the leaders finishing the conflict with the second highest total of 'kills', the lowest pilot loss rate and the longest serving squadron in the front line. The roll of Honour, proudly displayed in the Museum, records this momentous time in our nation's history. After a spell at Prestwick and Ayr in early 1941, 602 returned south flying strike sorties into Europe from Kenley and Redhill and later provided fighter cover during the Dieppe Raid in August 1942. In September the Squadron moved north to the Orkney and Shetland Islands to intercept the high level German reconnaissance raiders over Scapa Flow. It flew from bases in the south of England from January 1943 and transferred to the Second Tactical Air Force in November flying offensive sweeps over France and providing fighter escorts. Involved in the 'D' Day invasion, 602 later flew from airfields in Europe before returning to England in September 1944 to concentrate on strikes against V2 rocket sites and other prime targets. The Squadron disbanded on 15 May 1945 by which time it had been credited with the destruction of 150 enemy aircraft.

After the war 602 Squadron was reformed in its auxiliary status flying Spitfires from Abbotsinch (now Glasgow Airport) and, for a time, from Renfrew. The Spitfires gave way to Vampire jets in January 1951 which were flown until final disbandment in January 1957.

In 1941, Sir Patrick Dollan, then Lord Provost of Glasgow, wrote "Some day the City should provide a suitable memorial to the gallantry of the pilots of 602 Squadron" Some 40 years later, on learning of this statement and that nothing had been done, the Cadets of 2175 (Rolls-Royce) Squadron of the Air Training Corps accepted it as a challenge and within 18 months, with the help of many friends, established the Museum as a fitting tribute to the memory of this elite band of men.

Although not having any aircraft exhibits at present, the Museum houses many priceless artifacts and memorabilia including the Squadron Silverware, a Rolls-Royce Merlin engine, uniforms and decorations and medals, original drawings of 602 pilots by Cuthbert Orde, the Battle of Britain Memorial Book, a photo gallery, maps, paintings and reference books. It is located behind the 2175 (Rolls-Royce) Squadron Air Training Corps premises at Queen Elizabeth Avenue, Hillington, Glasgow.

Admission to the Museum is free but, as the Museum is entirely self-financing, any donations are greatly appreciated.

Associate Membership of the 602 Museum Association is available to anyone interested in the RAF in general and 602 in particular.

OPENING HOURS

As the Museum is manned by volunteers it's opening times are limited but access is usually available on Wednesday evenings between 7.30 and 9.30 pm and on the first Sunday of each month from April to September between 2.00 and 5.00 pm. Please check with the Museum Association secretary on 01505 862 225.

The Museum may also be opened by special arrangement by writing to:
The Chairman, 602 Museum Association,
c/o Rolls-Royce plc, Hillington, Glasgow G52 4TY

There are many souvenir items available for purchase including prints of squadron aircraft, postcards, bookmarks and badge pins & stickers.